2021

International Fuel Gas Code®

STUDY COMPANION

From the publisher of the IFGC®

Features:
- 10 study sessions and quizzes
- 250 total questions and answers
- Fully illustrated

A great learning tool for:
- Building inspectors
- Plans examiners
- Contractors

2021 *International Fuel Gas Code®*
Study Companion:
Based on the 2021 *International Fuel Gas Code®*

International Code Council Staff:

Executive Vice President and Director of Business Development:
 Mark A. Johnson

Senior Vice President, Business and Product Development
 Hamid Naderi

Vice President and Technical Director, Products and Services:
 Doug Thornburg

Senior Marketing Specialist:
 Dianna Hallmark

Manager of Product Development:
 Mary Lou Luif

Project Manager:
 Doug Thornburg

Publications Manager:
 Anne F. Kerr

Manager of Publications Production:
 Jen Fitzsimmons

Project Editor:
 Valerie Necka

Production Technician:
 Sandra Perkins

Cover Design:
 Ricky Razo

COPYRIGHT © 2021
by INTERNATIONAL CODE COUNCIL, INC.

ALL RIGHTS RESERVED.

ISBN: 978-1-955052-32-0 (soft-cover edition)
ISBN: 978-1-955052-33-7 (PDF download)

This publication is a copyrighted work owned by the International Code Council, Inc. ("ICC"). Without separate written permission from the ICC, no part of this publication may be reproduced, distributed or transmitted in any form or by any means, including, without limitation, electronic, optical or mechanical means (by way of example, and not limitation, photocopying or recording by or in an information storage and/or retrieval system). For information on use rights and permissions, please contact: ICC Publications, 4051 Flossmoor Road, Country Club Hills, Illinois 60478. Phone: 1-888-ICC-SAFE (422-7233).

The information contained in this document is believed to be accurate; however, it is being provided for informational purposes only and is intended for use only as a guide. Publication of this document by the ICC should not be construed as the ICC engaging in or rendering engineering, legal or other professional services. Use of the information contained in this publication should not be considered by the user as a substitute for the advice of a registered professional engineer, attorney or other professional. If such advice is required, it should be sought through the services of a registered professional engineer, licensed attorney or other professional.

Trademarks: "International Code Council," the "International Code Council" logo, "ICC," the "ICC" logo, "International Fuel Gas Code," "IFGC" and other names and trademarks appearing in this publication are registered trademarks of the International Code Council, Inc., and/or its licensors (as applicable), and may not be used without permission.

Errata on various ICC publications may be available at www.iccsafe.org/errata.

First Printing: July 2021

PRINTED IN THE USA

TABLE OF CONTENTS

Study Session 1:
  2021 IFGC Chapter 1—Scope and Administration 1
  Quiz 15

Study Session 2:
  2021 IFGC Sections 301 through 304—General Regulations I 21
  Quiz 35

Study Session 3:
  2021 IFGC Sections 305 through 310—General Regulations II 41
  Quiz 56

Study Session 4:
  2021 IFGC Sections 401 through 406—Gas Piping Installations I 63
  Quiz 78

Study Session 5:
  2021 IFGC Sections 407 through 416—Gas Piping Installations II 85
  Quiz 100

Study Session 6:
  2021 IFGC Sections 501 through 503.6.14—Chimneys and Vents I 107
  Quiz 126

Study Session 7:
  2021 IFGC Sections 503.7 through 506—Chimneys and Vents II 131
  Quiz 143

Study Session 8:
  2021 IFGC Sections 601 through 614—Specific Appliances I 149
  Quiz 164

Study Session 9:
  2021 IFGC Sections 615 through 635—Specific Appliances II 171
  Quiz 185

Study Session 10:
  2021 IFGC Chapter 7—Gaseous Hydrogen Systems 191
  Quiz 200

Answer Keys 205

INTRODUCTION

This study companion provides practical learning assignments for independent study of the provisions of the 2021 *International Fuel Gas Code*® (IFGC®). The independent study format affords a method for the student to complete the program in an unregulated time period. Progressing through the workbook, the learner can measure their level of knowledge by using the exercises and quizzes provided for each study session.

The workbook is also valuable for instructor-led programs. In jurisdictional training sessions, community college classes, vocational training programs and other structured educational offerings, the study guide and the IFGC can be the basis for classroom instruction.

All study sessions begin with a general learning objective specific to the session, the specific code sections or chapter under consideration and a list of questions summarizing the key points of study. Each session addresses selected topics from the IFGC and includes code text, a commentary on the code provisions, illustrations representing the provisions under discussion and multiple choice questions that can be used to evaluate the student's knowledge. Before beginning the quizzes, the student should thoroughly review the IFGC, focusing on the key points identified at the beginning of each study session.

The workbook is structured so that after every question the student has an opportunity to record their response and the corresponding code reference. The correct answers are found in the back of the workbook in the answer key.

Although this study companion is primarily focused on those subjects of specific interest to inspectors and contractors involved in fuel gas system installations, it is a valuable resource to any individuals who would like to learn more about the IFGC provisions. The information presented may be of importance to many building officials, plans examiners and combination inspectors.

This study companion was initially developed by Rudy Martinez, Mechanical Code Training Officer in the Department of Building and Safety for the City of Los Angeles. ICC staff provided assistance and updated the material to the successive editions. The 2021 *IFGC Study Companion* was updated by ICC staff members.

The information presented in this publication is believed to be accurate; however, it is provided for informational purposes only and is intended for use only as a guide. As there is a limited discussion of selected code provisions, the code itself should always be referenced for more complete information. In addition, the commentary set forth may not necessarily represent the views of any enforcing agency, as such agencies have the sole authority to render interpretations of the IFGC.

Questions or comments concerning this study companion are encouraged. Please direct your comments to ICC at studycompanion@iccsafe.org.

About the International Code Council®

The International Code Council is the leading global source of model codes and standards and building safety solutions that include product evaluation, accreditation, technology, codification, training and certification. The Code Council's codes, standards and solutions are used to ensure safe, affordable and sustainable communities and buildings worldwide. The International Code Council family of solutions includes the ICC Evaluation Service, the International Accreditation Service, General Code, S. K. Ghosh Associates, NTA Inc., ICC Community Development Solutions and the Alliance for National & Community Resilience. The Code Council is the largest international association of building safety professionals and is the trusted source of model codes and standards, establishing the baseline for building safety globally and creating a level playing field for designers, builders and manufacturers.

Washington DC Headquarters:

500 New Jersey Avenue, NW, 6th Floor, Washington, DC 20001

Regional Offices:

Eastern Regional Office (BIR)
Central Regional Office (CH)
Western Regional Office (LA)

Distribution Center (Lenexa, KS)

888-ICC-SAFE (888-422-7233)

www.iccsafe.org

Family of Solutions:

2021 IFGC Chapter 1
Scope and Administration

OBJECTIVE: To gain an understanding of the administrative portions of the IFGC, including the enforcement responsibilities of the code official and the various tools available to enforce the code.

REFERENCE: Chapter 1, 2021 *International Fuel Gas Code*

KEY POINTS:
- Which type of occupancies are regulated by the IFGC?
- Which type of fuel is regulated to a maximum pressure of 125 pounds per square inch?
- Which types of fuel systems are outside the scope of the IFGC?
- What is the intent of the IFGC in regard to minimum standards?
- When there is a conflict between a general requirement and a specific requirement, which requirement takes precedence?
- How is existing work regulated, considering the protection through non-conforming rights?
- What requirements apply to maintenance of existing equipment?
- When an addition, alteration or renovation takes place, is the existing installation required to conform to the new code requirements?
- What process must be followed when there is a change of occupancy in an existing building?
- Under what conditions are historical buildings exempt from code requirements?
- What are the powers and duties of the code official in regard to application and interpretation of the code?
- Is the code official required to make all inspections?
- If the code official believes an unsafe condition exists, can the code official enter a building without the owner's permission?
- What are modifications and how do they apply?

KEY POINTS:
(Cont'd)

- How may alternative materials, designs and methods of construction be approved? What action is required when a proposed alternative material or method of construction is not approved?
- What is a Research Report, and how is it used?
- When an appliance does not have the required approvals for installation, what are the options for gaining compliance with the code?
- What must be done before work on a room addition can commence on any building regulated by the IFGC?
- When installing a portable heating appliance, is a permit required?
- What time limits apply to permit applications and issued permits?
- What construction documents are required to obtain a permit? Are construction documents required to be kept at the job site for review by the building official?
- Is the permit or copy of the permit required to be kept at the job site?
- Under what circumstances can the code official authorize temporary connection of utilities before a final inspection has been approved?
- What authority does the code official have to condemn installations? Under what circumstances?
- What must occur before the code official orders disconnection of service utilities?

Topic: Scope
Reference: IFGC 101.2

Category: Scope and Administration
Subject: General Requirements

Code Text: *This code shall apply to the installation of fuel gas piping systems, fuel gas appliances, gaseous hydrogen systems and related accessories in accordance with Sections 101.2.1 through 101.2.5.* **Exception:** *Detached one- and two-family dwellings and townhouses not more than three stories above grade plane in height with separate means of egress and their accessory structures not more than three stories above grade plane in height, shall comply with this code or the* International Residential Code.

Discussion and Commentary: The IFGC regulates the installation of fuel gas systems, including gas piping, appliances, equipment and related components. The fuel gas being utilized in these systems may be natural gas, liquefied petroleum gas (LP-gas), hydrogen gas, manufactured gas or some mixture of these gases. Certain portable systems, industrial applications and gas supplier installations are outside the scope of the code, as are liquefied and compressed natural gas (LNG and CNG) systems. The applicability of the code spans from the initial design of fuel gas systems through the installation and construction phases, and includes operation and maintenance of fuel gas systems.

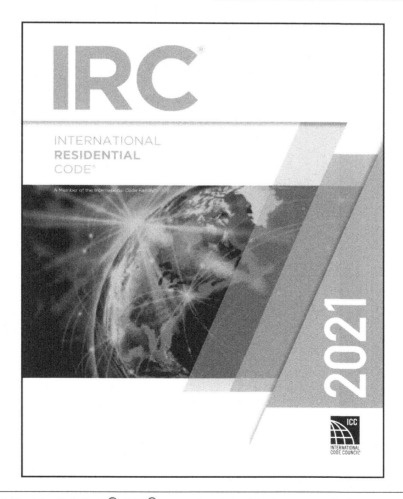

The *International Residential Code*® (IRC®) was developed to be a stand alone code for one- and two-family dwellings and town homes including provisions for fuel gas systems. The applicable provisions of the IFGC and Chapter 24 of the IRC are identical.

Topic: Piping Systems
Reference: IFGC 101.2.2

Category: Scope and Administration
Subject: General Requirements

Code Text: *These regulations cover piping systems for natural gas with an operating pressure of 125 psig or less, and for LP-gas with an operating pressure of 20 psig or less, except as provided in Section 402.7. Coverage shall extend from the point of delivery to the outlet of the appliance shutoff valves. Piping system requirements shall include design, materials, components, fabrication, installation, testing, inspection, operation and maintenance.*

Discussion and Commentary: Depending on the selected fuel gas, the IFGC is applicable to piping systems that operate within a prescribed range of pressure limits. The code also places other limitations on gas pressures and provides for increased LP-gas pressures in Section 402.7. In addition to pressure limits, the design, materials, components, fabrication, installation, operation and maintenance of piping systems fall within the scope of the code as well.

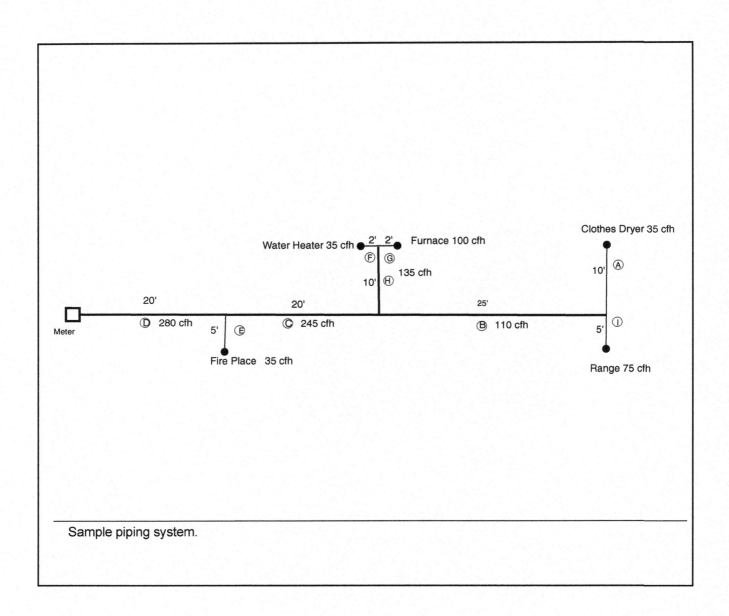

Sample piping system.

Topic: Appendices
Reference: IFGC 101.3
Category: Scope and Administration
Subject: General Requirements

Code Text: *Provisions in the appendices shall not apply unless specifically adopted.*

Discussion and Commentary: Appendices are not part of the body of the code and cannot be enforced unless specifically adopted in the ordinance of the local jurisdiction. Information in the appendix chapters is considered outside the scope and purpose of the traditional code provisions at the time of publication. The information may also be specialized and applicable to only a limited number of installations. Appendix chapters or portions thereof that gain general acceptance over time are sometimes moved into the main body of the code through the code development process.

IFGC Appendices

Appendix A
SIZING AND CAPACITIES OF GAS PIPING

Appendix B
SIZING OF VENTING SYSTEMS SERVING
APPLIANCES EQUIPPED WITH DRAFT HOODS,
CATEGORY 1 APPLIANCES AND APPLIANCES
LISTED FOR USE WITH TYPE B VENTS

Appendix C
EXIT TERMINALS OF MECHANICAL DRAFT AND
DIRECT - VENTING SYSTEMS

Appendix D
RECOMMENDED PROCEDURE FOR SAFETY
INSPECTION OF AN EXISTING APPLIANCE
INSTALLATION

Appendix E
BOARD OF APPEALS

Appendices not adopted by the jurisdiction may still have useful information such as tables, configurations and formulas that are of value in the application of the code. For example, provisions in the appendices may provide some degree of assistance in evaluating proposed alternative designs, methods or materials in the installation of fuel gas systems.

Topic: General Provisions	Category: Scope and Administration
Reference: IFGC 102.1	Subject: Applicability

Code Text: *Where there is a conflict between a general requirement and a specific requirement, the specific requirement shall govern. Where, in a specific case, different sections of this code specify different materials, methods of construction or other requirements, the most restrictive shall govern.*

Discussion and Commentary: Inevitably, there are provisions in different sections of the code that appear to be in conflict. The IFGC prescribes two methods to resolve these apparent differences. In the first, the code official must determine which of the conflicting requirements is more specific in applying the provision of the code. In the second, when different materials or methods are prescribed for the specific installation, the most restrictive code requirement applies.

The code official is assigned broad authority by the code to use good judgment in making determinations and interpretations in fulfilling the intent and purpose of the code. When conflicts occur in the code, the code official is directed to enforce the more specific and the more restrictive requirements.

Topic: Existing Installations	**Category:** Scope and Administration
Reference: IFGC 102.2	**Subject:** Applicability

Code Text: *Except as otherwise provided for in this chapter, a provision in this code shall not require the removal, alteration or abandonment of, nor prevent the continued utilization and maintenance of, existing installations lawfully in existence at the time of the adoption of this code.*

Discussion and Commentary: New work, including repairs, alterations and additions to existing systems, must comply with all code requirements. However, existing installations that have been installed legally but do not conform to the latest code are not required to be brought into compliance, provided the system is properly maintained and reasonably safe. Such installations may continue to be used without modification. In the case of an addition or alteration to an existing system, only the new work is required to comply with the code, provided the addition or alteration does not cause the existing system to become unsafe or overloaded. Minor alterations and repairs may be approved when installed in the same manner as the existing system in accordance with Section 102.4.

Work related to the structural aspects of an existing building must comply with the IBC.

Topic: Maintenance
Reference: IFGC 102.3

Category: Scope and Administration
Subject: Applicability

Code Text: *Installations, both existing and new, and parts thereof shall be maintained in proper operating condition in accordance with the original design and in a safe condition. Devices or safeguards which are required by this code shall be maintained in compliance with the code edition under which they were installed. The owner or the owner's authorized agent shall be responsible for maintenance of installations. To determine compliance with this provision, the code official shall have the authority to require an installation to be re-inspected.*

Discussion and Commentary: Mechanical systems are subject to normal wear and tear that over time may impair the intended function of the system or cause an unsafe condition. Therefore, the IFGC requires installations to be maintained to operate properly. Consistent with the provisions granting grandfather rights to legal nonconforming installations, existing equipment need only be maintained to comply with the code in effect at the time of installation. The code official has the authority to re-inspect premises to verify appropriate maintenance and to require correction if a condition exists that is unsafe or a hazard to health, property or public welfare.

Notice of Inspection
City of _____

Date _____
Address of Job _____
Existing Permit   yes   no
Reason for Inspection _____
_____
_____
_____
_____
_____

Requested Date _____
Alternate Date _____

_____
Code Official

The code official is obligated to notify the owner or the owner's agent of the request to inspect the premises. A written request, sometimes called a "gain entry letter" is recommended.

Topic: Change in Occupancy	**Category:** Scope and Administration
Reference: IFGC 102.5	**Subject:** Applicability

Code Text: *It shall be unlawful to make a change in the occupancy of a structure which will subject the structure to the special provisions of this code applicable to the new occupancy without approval. The code official shall certify that such structure meets the intent of the provisions of law governing building construction for the proposed new occupancy and that such change of occupancy does not result in any hazard to the public health, safety or welfare.*

Discussion and Commentary: When a building undergoes a change of occupancy, requirements for fuel gas systems may also change. The code official is responsible for determining if the change in the use of the building subjects existing fuel gas installations to the special provisions of the IFGC or creates any unsafe conditions. In addition, any new work related to the change in occupancy, such as the installation of kitchen equipment when converting from an office space to a restaurant use, must be installed in accordance with the codes in effect at the time the permit is issued.

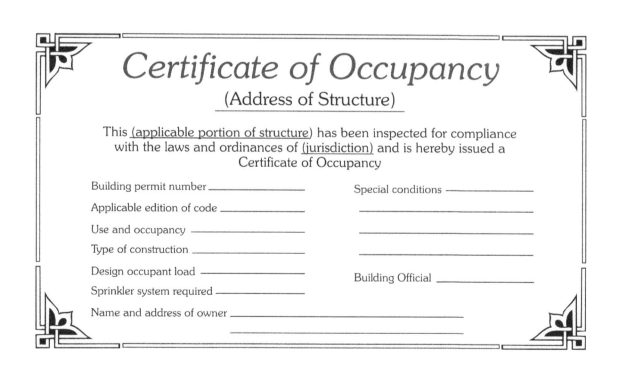

The above illustration is an example of a certificate of occupancy that is required by the IBC before a building or portion thereof can be used or occupied.

Topic: Inspections
Reference: IFGC 104.3
Category: Scope and Administration
Subject: Duties and Powers of the Code Official

Code Text: *The code official shall make all the required inspections, or shall accept reports of inspection by approved agencies or individuals. All reports of such inspections shall be in writing and shall be certified by a responsible officer of such approved agency or by the responsible individual. the code official is authorized to engage such expert opinion as deemed necessary to report upon unusual technical issues that arise, subject to the approval of the appointing authority.*

Discussion and Commentary: The inspection process is critical to ensuring that the work is in compliance with the code so as to protect the public health, safety and welfare. Typically, inspections are carried out by the building safety department in stages as the work progresses and before any work is covered up. As an alternative, the code official is authorized to accept reports of inspection from other approved sources. Certain installations may require the expertise of a specialist, who may have pertinent knowledge or skills that are outside the area of expertise of the inspection department personnel. These expert opinions may be obtained from various sources such as another code official who has years of experience in a particular field or an engineer who specializes in the applicable installation.

MECHANICAL INSPECTION RECORD

CITY OF ANYTOWN

PERMIT NUMBER _____

ADDRESS _____

_____

_____

CONTRACTOR, IF APPLICABLE _____

NO WORK IS TO BE COVERED PRIOR TO INSPECTION AND APPROVAL

UNDERGROUND, UNDERFLOOR

☐ APPROVED DATE _____

ROUGH-IN

☐ APPROVED DATE _____

FINAL

☐ APPROVED DATE _____

OTHERS _____ DATE _____

_____ DATE _____

_____ DATE _____

The code official is required to maintain official records, including the results of inspections. Usually, a record of inspection is displayed at the job site and recorded electronically on a computer or written on a paper form for inclusion in the permanent file of the department.

Topic: Modifications
Reference: IFGC 105.1
Category: Scope and Administration
Subject: Approval

Code Text: *Where there are practical difficulties involved in carrying out the provisions of this code, the code official shall have the authority to grant modifications for individual cases, upon application of the owner or owner's authorized agent, provided that the code official shall first find that special individual reason makes the strict letter of this code impractical and that such modification is in compliance with the intent and purpose of this code and does not lessen health, life, and fire safety requirements. The details of action granting modifications shall be recorded and entered in the files of the Department of Inspection.*

Discussion and Commentary: The intent of the provisions allowing modification of the code is to give the builder a means to complete an installation when following the strict letter of the code is not possible or realistic. If an alternate means can be accomplished without lessening the health, life and fire safety aspects of the building, then a modification may be given. The code official is required to record all instances of granting a modification and to include the reasons for the modification.

REQUEST AND APPROVAL FOR CODE MODIFICATION

DATE _____

ADDRESS _____
_____

PERMIT NUMBER _____

APPLICABLE CODE SECTION (S) _____
_____

REASON INSTALLATION CANNOT COMPLY WITH CODE PROVISION _____
_____

DOES MODIFICATION MEET THE INTENT AND PURPOSE OF THE CODE? _____
_____

DOES IT MEET THE HEALTH, LIFE, AND FIRE SAFETY REQUIREMENTS? _____
_____

REQUEST APPROVED   YES   NO

REASON _____
_____

_____
Mechanical Code Official

As long as there is a valid justification approved by the jurisdiction, a modification can be a useful tool in allowing safe installations that do not otherwise fully comply with the code provisions.

Topic: Research Reports
Reference: IFGC 105.2.1
Category: Scope and Administration
Subject: Approval

Code Text: Supporting data, where necessary to assist in the approval of materials or assemblies not specifically provided for in this code, shall consist of valid research reports from approved sources.

Discussion and Commentary: The code does not limit the use of materials and methods to only those prescribed. It recognizes that innovation and technological advances in the installation of fuel gas systems occur on a regular basis. In the absence of specific provisions addressing particular materials or assemblies, the code official is authorized to require a research report from an approved source, such as ICC Evaluation Service (ES). An ICC ES report presents findings as to the compliance with code requirements of the material or component evaluated.

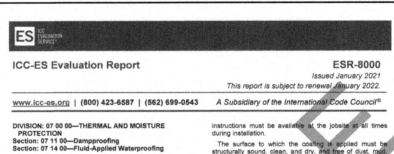

ICC Evaluation Service (ES) Reports maintained by ICC Evaluation Service, Inc. are valuable tools for determining compliance with the code for alternative methods and materials. ICC ES reports are developed based upon acceptance criteria for products to verify performance equivalent to that prescribed by the code.

Topic: Permits Required
Reference: IFGC 106.1
Category: Scope and Administration
Subject: Permits

Code Text: *An owner, owner's authorized agent or contractor who desires to erect, install, enlarge, alter, repair, remove, convert or replace an installation regulated by this code, or to cause such work to be done, shall first make application to the code official and obtain the required permit for the work.*

Exception: Where appliance and equipment replacements and repairs are required to be performed in an emergency situation, the permit application shall be submitted within the next working business day of the Department of Inspection.

Discussion and Commentary: For other than portable heating appliances and replacement of minor components, installations related to fuel gas systems require a permit before any work takes place. Such work is subject to subsequent inspections at periodic intervals throughout the course of construction. In an emergency situation, the work may take place before obtaining a permit, but the permit is still required to be obtained in a timely manner.

MECHANICAL PERMIT
City of _____

PERMIT NUMBER _____

DATE ISSUED _____

CONTRACTOR _____

HOMEOWNER _____

DESCRIPTION OF WORK _____

NEW   EXISTING/REPAIR   REPLACEMENT

REQUIRED INSPECTIONS _____

FEES _____

_____
Mechanical Code Official

24 HOURS NOTICE REQUIRED

A permit provides a written record of the location and scope of the work, the occupancy of the building, the name of the owner and other pertinent information as required by the code official. Inspection results, notices, correspondence and final approval become a part of the permanent permit record.

Topic: Permits Not Required
Reference: IFGC 106.2

Category: Scope and Administration
Subject: Permits

Code Text: *Permits shall not be required for the following: (1) Any portable heating appliance, (2) Replacement of any minor component of an appliance or equipment that does not alter approval of such appliance or equipment or make such appliance or equipment unsafe.*

Exemption from the permit requirements of this code shall not be deemed to grant authorization for work to be done in violation of the provisions of this code or of other laws or ordinances of this jurisdiction.

Discussion and Commentary: Generally, work on any portion of a fuel gas system requires a permit and is subject to inspections. The code exempts the installation of portable heating appliances and the replacement of minor components from the permit requirements. Though not defined, a portable heating appliance may be a heater that is not attached to the building structure, has a self-contained portable fuel gas supply and may be connected to a power source with an electrical cord and plug connection. What defines a portable heating appliance rests with the code official. Portable LP-gas appliances that are not connected to a fixed fuel gas piping system are not regulated by the code.

Whether or not a permit is required by the code, all installations must be in accordance with the code requirements. The owner is responsible for proper and safe installations.

Quiz

Study Session 1
IFGC Chapter 1

1. Fuel gas installations in detached one- and two-family dwellings and multiple single-family dwellings (townhouses) not more than three stories in height with separate means of egress must comply with the _____.

    a. *International Fuel Gas Code* (IFGC)

    b. *International Building Code* (IBC)

    c. *International Residential Code* (IRC)

    d. *International Mechanical Code* (IMC)

    Reference_____

2. The IFGC regulates piping systems for natural gas with an operating pressure of _____ psig or less.

    a. 125
    b. 90
    c. 5
    d. 20

    Reference_____

3. The IFGC does not apply to_____.

    a. LP-gas piping systems

    b. gaseous hydrogen systems

    c. oxygen-fuel gas cutting systems

    d. gas appliance ventilation air

    Reference_____

4. The purpose of this code is to provide _____ standards to safeguard life or limb, health, property and public welfare.

   a. minimum
   b. maximum
   c. consensus
   d. acceptable

   Reference_____

5. Where, in a specific case, different sections of the code specify different materials, methods of construction or other requirements, the _____ requirement shall apply.

   a. general
   b. most restrictive
   c. specific
   d. least restrictive

   Reference_____

6. An installation is not required to be brought into compliance if it is _____ at the time of adoption of the code.

   a. listed
   b. labeled
   c. operational
   d. lawfully in existence

   Reference_____

7. The _____ shall be responsible for the maintenance of fuel gas installations.

   a. contractor that services the equipment
   b. occupant of the structure
   c. code authority
   d. owner or owner's authorized agent

   Reference_____

8. An addition to a fuel gas installation shall conform to that required for _____ installations.

   a. existing
   b. new
   c. modified
   d. relocated

   Reference_____

9. When the provisions of the IFGC are applicable, a change of occupancy requires _____.
    a. a permit
    b. a certificate of occupancy
    c. approval
    d. inspection
    Reference_____

10. Provided there are no unsafe conditions, classified _____ buildings are exempt from the provisions of the code.
    a. historic
    b. police department
    c. public
    d. fire department
    Reference_____

11. Where the code official finds that a proposed alternative material does not comply with the intent of the code provisions, the code official shall _____.
    a. request additional information from the manufacturer
    b. state the reason for disapproval in writing to the applicant
    c. contact a third-party agency to authorize additional testing
    d. place limitations on the use of the alternative material
    Reference_____

12. The code official is authorized to accept reports of inspection by_____.
    a. specialized contractors
    b. approved agencies or individuals
    c. registered design professionals
    d. special inspectors
    Reference_____

13. The code official has the authority to _____ the provisions of the code.
    a. waive
    b. interpret
    c. ignore
    d. violate
    Reference_____

14. The code official has the authority to grant modifications to the code _____.

    a. only for those issues not affecting fire and life safety
    b. where the intent and purpose of the code cannot be met
    c. only when related to administrative functions
    d. for individual cases where the strict letter of the code is impractical

    Reference _____

15. Alternative methods or materials not specifically prescribed by the code are permitted when _____.

    a. designed by a registered design professional
    b. tested
    c. approved
    d. listed

    Reference _____

16. _____ provide supporting documentation to verify that an alternative material or assembly complies with the intent of the code.

    a. Research reports
    b. Manufacturer's installation instructions
    c. Inspection reports
    d. Construction documents

    Reference _____

17. Tests performed by _____ may be required by the code official where there is insufficient evidence of code compliance.

    a. the owner
    b. an approved agency
    c. the contractor
    d. a design professional

    Reference _____

18. The _____ is not required on an application for a permit.
    a. proposed occupancy   b. description of work
    c. location of work   d. type of construction
    Reference_____

19. A permit is not required for installation of a _____.
    a. horizontal furnace   b. portable heating appliance
    c. heat pump system   d. vented gas fireplace
    Reference_____

20. If the permit has not been issued, an application for a permit is considered abandoned _____ days after the date of filing.
    a. 30   b. 60
    c. 90   d. 180
    Reference_____

21. One set of approved construction documents shall be kept _____ while work is in progress.
    a. with the registered design professional
    b. by the owner of the building
    c. at the job site
    d. with the contractor
    Reference_____

22. The permit or a copy shall be kept on the site of the work _____.
    a. until the completion of the project
    b. until the work commences
    c. until a certificate of occupancy is issued
    d. for one year after the work is completed
    Reference_____

23. The code official has the authority to allow temporary connection of an installation to the sources of energy for the purpose of_____.

    a. construction
    b. heating
    c. lighting
    d. testing

    Reference_____

24. Which of the following individuals is not qualified to serve on the Board of Appeals for the IFGC?

    a. A registered design professional who is a registered architect
    b. A registered design professional with fuel gas and plumbing engineering experience
    c. An electrical contractor with at least 10 years of experience, 5 of which the contractor was responsible for the work
    d. Employee of the jurisdiction

    Reference_____

25. Only in an emergency situation that poses an immediate hazard to life or property is the code official authorized to_____.

    a. require disconnection of utility service
    b. declare the installation unsafe
    c. condemn the installation
    d. post a stop work order

    Reference_____

2021 IFGC Sections 301 through 304
General Regulations I

OBJECTIVE: To develop an understanding of the general code provisions related to the listing and labeling of appliances, the types of fuel gas, the protection of the structure and the installation of appliances including combustion air requirements.

REFERENCE: Sections 301 through 304, 2021 *International Fuel Gas Code*

KEY POINTS:
- What is the basis for accepting appliances?
- What procedures are used for labeling appliances?
- Who must test a representative sample of the appliances being labeled?
- What minimum qualifications apply to a testing agency?
- What restrictions apply to cuts, notches and holes bored in engineered wood products?
- What are the maximum sizes and location restrictions of notches and bored holes in solid wood joists and studs?
- Under what conditions are alterations of trusses permitted?
- In which locations are direct vent appliances permitted where other appliances generally are prohibited?
- What locations require protection of appliances against vehicle impact? What is the minimum protection required?
- Under what conditions is an appliance permitted to be installed in a closet?
- What requirements apply to appliances installed in a pit or excavation?
- A draft hood or a barometric regulator must be installed in what location?
- What is the remedy when an exhaust fan interferes with the operation of an appliance?
- What is the standard method used for calculating indoor combustion air?
- How is the air infiltration rate of a structure used for calculating the amount of required combustion air?

KEY POINTS:
(Cont'd)
- How is the minimum size of a combustion air opening determined?
- How are the combustion air requirements determined when obtaining combustion air from more than one story?
- Where must combustion air openings be located?
- Under what circumstances is a single opening permitted for obtaining combustion air?
- When is a mechanical combustion air system permitted?
- When is an appliance interlock system required for obtaining combustion air?
- How is the net free area determined for louvers and grilles that cover combustion air openings?
- What are the material and construction requirements for combustion air ducts?
- How many appliance enclosures may be served by a combustion air duct?
- Is a single duct permitted to serve both the upper and lower combustion air openings?
- What are the clearance requirements for combustion air intake openings?

Topic: Listed and Labeled
Reference: IFGC 301.3

Category: General Regulations
Subject: General Requirements

Code Text: *Appliances regulated by this code shall be listed and labeled for the application in which they are used unless otherwise approved in accordance with Section 105. The approval of unlisted appliances in accordance with Section 105 shall be based upon approved engineering evaluation.*

Discussion and Commentary: Listing and labeling of an appliance in accordance with the IFGC assures the code official that the appliance has been tested to operate safely for the intended use. Testing is performed by an approved independent agency in accordance with the relevant standards. The approved testing agency must have appropriate equipment, employ experienced personnel and maintain detailed records of all tests performed. In addition to providing a reliable basis for approval, an appliance label contains important information related to its safe installation and operation.

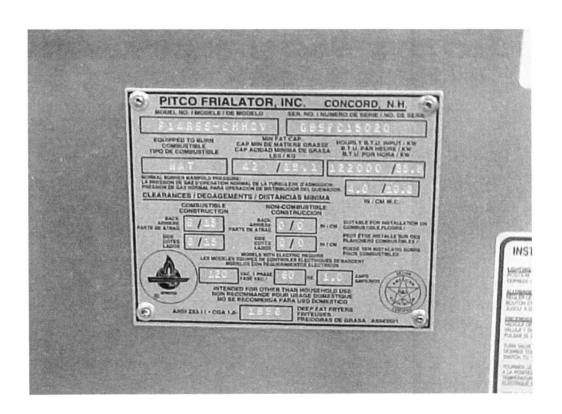

The code official has the authority to approve unlisted appliances, but the approval must be based on an engineering evaluation. Such an evaluation may be based on testing by an approved independent testing agency.

Topic: Label Information	**Category:** General Regulations
Reference: IFGC 301.5	**Subject:** General Requirements

Code Text: *A permanent factory-applied nameplate(s) shall be affixed to appliances on which shall appear in legible lettering, the manufacturer's name or trademark, the model number, serial number and, for listed appliances, the seal or mark of the testing agency. A label shall also include the hourly rating in British thermal units per hour (Btu/h) (W); the type of fuel approved for use with the appliance; and the minimum clearance requirements.*

Discussion and Commentary: The required label provides information for the safe installation, operation and maintenance of an appliance. The required information includes the

1. manufacturer's name or trademark,
2. model number,
3. serial number,
4. name and trademark of the approved listing agency,
5. hourly Btu rating,
6. type of fuel, and
7. minimum clearance requirements.

```
                                    Air Conditioning Co.
                                    La Habra Ca. 90631
       CREATIVE                     Made in USA
      TESTING LAB
                       Forced Air Furnace         Category I
                       ANS Z21.47 - 1990    CENTRAL FURNACE
                       FOR INDOOR INSTALLATION IN A BUILDING
                       CONSTRUCTED ON SITE              MCJL
MODEL NO.          SERIAL NO.          EQUIPPED FOR
LEA 6902480        CAS 4402421         JEN.        GAS
INPUT              LIMIT SETTING
  80,000   BTU/HR  190                 JONAH,      12/08
TEMP RISE          MAX.EX.STATIC PRESS MAX DESIGN AIR
FROM   30 TO 60    .50INCHES OF WATER  TEMP 160° F
VOLTS/PHASE/HERT   TOTAL AMPS          MAX.DESIGN AIR
115/1/60           8.5                   1 SON

    MANIFOLD PRESSURE         FLAME ROLLOUT SWITCH - REPLACE
    (INCHES OF WATER)         IF BLOWN WITH CATALOG NO.
    NAT. 3.5                  WG09X033    (333 F CUTOFF TEMP.)
                              ONE TIME THERMAL FUSE
    SUPPLY PRESSURE
    (IN INCHES OF WATER)
    MAX. NAT. 10.5, LP 13.0
    MIN. NAT.   4.5 LP 11.0 FOR PURPOSE OF INPUT ADJUSTMENT.

           LOW INPUT 52,000 BTU/HR

    MINIMUM CLEARANCE COMBUSTIBLES
    FOR      CLOSET    INSTALLATION AS FOLLOWS:
    SIDES      0       IN. W/SINGLE WALL VENT
    FLUE       6       IN. W/SINGLE WALL VENT  1 IN / TYPE B-1
    VENT
    FRONT      6       IN.        BACK  0  IN   TOP  1  IN.
```

The appliance label is required to be a permanent nameplate such as a metal plate, tag or other permanent label attached to the appliance in an approved manner at the factory.

Topic: Appliance Fuel Conversion
Reference: IFGC 301.7.1
Category: General Regulations
Subject: General Requirements

Code Text: *Appliances shall not be converted to utilize a different fuel gas except where complete instructions for such conversion are provided in the installations instructions, by the serving gas supplier or by the appliance manufacturer.*

Discussion and Commentary: Appliances are designed and manufactured based on the specific properties of the fuel gas, and the appliance will not operate properly when supplied with a different type of fuel. Many manufacturers anticipate possible conversion to different types of fuel gas and provide instructions or components for safe conversion. The installer is required to follow the manufacturer's or the gas supplier's procedures for making the conversion. In the absence of such instructions, the code does not permit converting to a fuel other than the type for which the appliance is designed.

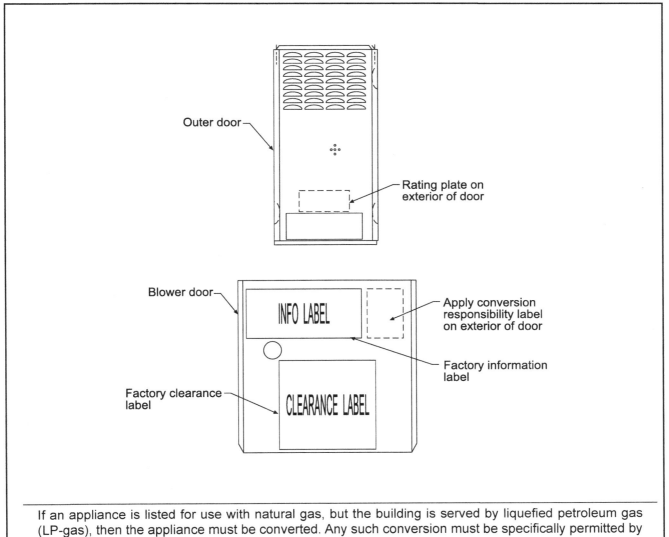

If an appliance is listed for use with natural gas, but the building is served by liquefied petroleum gas (LP-gas), then the appliance must be converted. Any such conversion must be specifically permitted by the listing of the appliance and the manufacturer. Connecting LP-gas to an appliance designed for use with natural gas creates a hazardous condition.

Topic: Engineered Wood Products
Reference: IFGC 302.3.1
Category: General Regulations
Subject: Structural Safety

Code Text: *Cuts, notches and holes bored in trusses, structural composite lumber, structural glued-laminated members and I-joists are prohibited except where permitted by the manufacturer's recommendations or where the effects of such alterations are specifically considered in the design of the member by a registered design professional.*

Discussion and Commentary: Engineered wood products include plate-connected open-web trusses, I-joists, laminated veneer lumber beams and headers, and other manufactured structural components that must be installed in accordance with the manufacturer's instructions. Some products, such as I-joists, are designed to accommodate the cutting or boring of holes of a limited size in specific locations as instructed by the manufacturer. On the other hand, trusses and laminated beams typically cannot be notched, cut or bored without an engineered design for the particular modification.

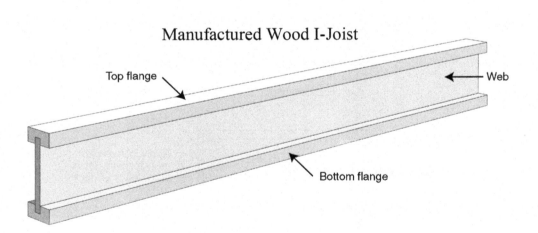

Manufactured Wood I-Joist

Do not drill, cut or notch flanges.
Use the manufacturer's web knockouts whenever possible.
Follow the manufacturer's instructions for cutting holes in the web.

By including the provisions for cutting, notching and boring of wood members in the IFGC, installers are likely to be more aware of their responsibilities in protecting the structural integrity of the building during the fuel gas system installation.

Topic: Stud Cutting and Notching
Reference: IFGC 302.3.3
Category: General Regulations
Subject: Structural Safety

Code Text: *In exterior walls and bearing partitions, any wood stud is permitted to be cut or notched to a depth not exceeding 25 percent of its width. Cutting or notching of studs to a depth not greater than 40 percent of the width of the stud is permitted in nonload-bearing partitions supporting no loads other than the weight of the partition.*

Discussion and Commentary: The installation of fuel gas systems and components must be accomplished without having an adverse effect on the structural integrity of the building components. For conventional solid-sawn-lumber framing members, the code establishes prescriptive size and location limitations for cuts, notches and bored holes. Cutting and notching is permitted in wood studs of exterior or bearing partitions, provided the cut or notch does not exceed 25 percent of the stud's width. For nonload bearing partitions, cutting and notching can be increased to 40 percent of the width. Exceeding these limits would compromise the structural integrity of the building. When cutting, notching or boring in studs, care must be taken by the installer not to exceed the prescribed limits.

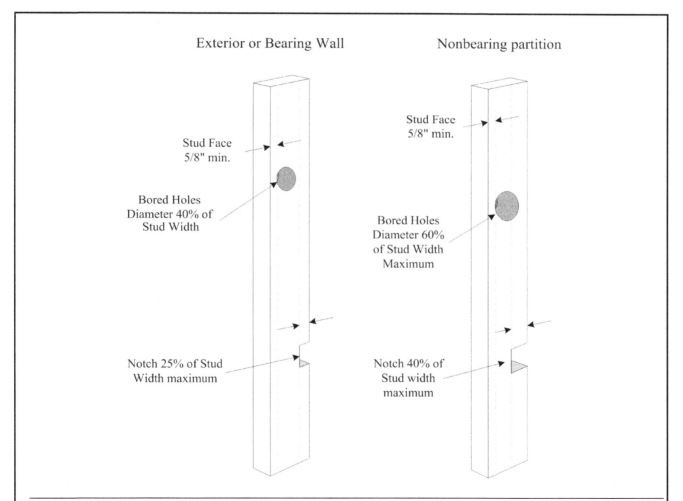

Section 302.3.4 permits bored holes in studs to be somewhat larger than cuts or notches, provided the holes maintain a minimum $5/8$-inch clearance to the edge of the stud. Bored hole diameters of 40 percent or less of the stud width are not considered to adversely affect the structural capability of the wood stud in any wall. Greater diameters are permitted under limited circumstances.

Topic: Prohibited Locations
Reference: IFGC 303.3
Category: General Regulations
Subject: Appliance Location

Code Text: *Appliances shall not be located in sleeping rooms, bathrooms, toilet rooms, storage closets or surgical rooms, or in a space that opens only into such rooms or spaces, except where the installation complies with one of the following:* See the list of six separate conditions permitting the installation of appliances in the above locations.

Discussion and Commentary: The code prohibits gas appliances in locations where people are most vulnerable to the effects of a malfunction or incomplete combustion. This is particularly important in bedrooms, for example, where occupants are most at risk when they are asleep and unaware of their surroundings. In addition, the code recognizes an increased risk from malfunctioning appliances in small confined spaces such as bathrooms or toilet rooms. In the case of a storage closet, the primary concern is that prescribed clearances around the appliance will not be maintained, preventing the appliance from operating properly or causing a fire hazard. The exceptions permit direct-vent appliances and appliances that are otherwise isolated from the described spaces. Consideration is also given to small heating and decorative appliances.

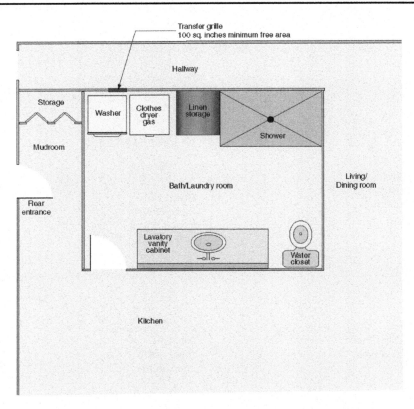

A gas clothes dryer is permitted in a bathroom where a permanent opening is installed for ventilation/makeup air.

An exception permits a gas-fired clothes dryer to be located in a bathroom or toilet room when a transfer opening is provided for ventilation and makeup air. The opening must have an area of at least 100 square inches and cannot communicate with a bedroom, bathroom, toilet room or closet (see Exception 6).

Topic: Standard Method
Category: General Regulations
Reference: IFGC 304.5.1
Subject: Combustion, Ventilation and Dilution Air

Code Text: *The minimum required volume shall be 50 cubic feet per 1,000 Btu/h (4.8 m³/kW) of the appliance input rating.*

Discussion and Commentary: Combustion air is required for proper operation of fuel-burning appliances and may be obtained from indoors, provided the necessary volume of air is available or may be obtained from outdoors. The standard method for providing indoor combustion air has been around for many years and is still widely used and accepted. Because determining the air changes per hour (ACH) requires a blower door or similar test, the ACH rate typically is not known and the standard method is deemed reliable for supplying adequate indoor combustion air without further calculations.

This equation has been used by inspectors for many years to determine if the appliance installed in a room has enough combustion air for proper operation

20 x the volume of the room = maximum BTUs of the appliance
1,000 btu/h divided by 50 cubic feet/h = 20 btu/cubic foot

If the building has been tested to determine an ACH rate and the ACH is less than 0.40, the standard method for calculating indoor combustion air is not permitted. In this case, the amount of indoor combustion air must be calculated using the known air-infiltration-rate method.

Topic: Known Air Infiltration Rate Method
Reference: IFGC 304.5.2
Category: General Regulations
Subject: Combustion, Ventilation and Dilution Air

Code Text: *Where the air infiltration rate of a structure is known, the minimum required volume shall be determined as follows:*

For appliances other than fan-assisted, calculate volume using Equation 3-1.
For fan-assisted appliances, calculate volume using Equation 3-2.
For purposes of this calculation, an infiltration rate greater than 0.60 ACH shall not be used in Equations 3-1 and 3-2.

Discussion and Commentary: There is no reliable method for predicting or estimating the air infiltration rate of a building without performing a blower door test. This test depressurizes the interior of the building to create a pressure differential with the outdoor air and measures the air leakage rate to determine the average air changes per hour (ACH). If testing determines that the ACH is less than 0.40 and combustion air is obtained from the indoors, the code requires that the volume of indoor air must be calculated using the known air-infiltration-rate method. There are two equations listed in this section for determining the required volume of indoor combustion air. The first provides a calculation for appliances having a gravity type of venting system, and the second provides a calculation for fan-assisted venting systems.

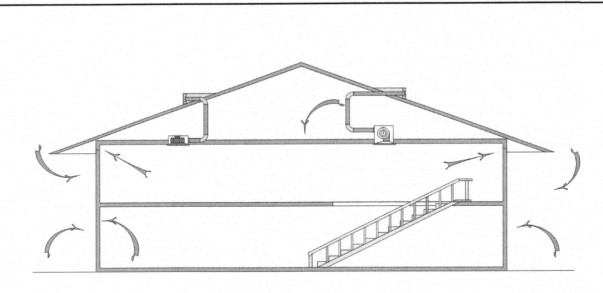

Air Infiltration in Buildings

The provisions for calculating the volume of indoor combustion air based on a known air infiltration rate anticipate relatively tight construction with a lower ACH. If the ACH is greater than 0.60, then air leakage is fairly significant and the air-infiltration-rate method is not appropriate.

Topic: Opening Size and Location
Reference: IFGC 304.5.3.1
Category: General Regulations
Subject: Combustion, Ventilation and Dilution Air

Code Text: *Where combining spaces on the same story, each opening shall have a minimum free area of 1 square inch per 1,000 Btu/h (2,200 mm^2/kW) of the total input rating of all appliances in the space, but not less than 100 square inches (0.06 m^2). One permanent opening shall commence within 12 inches (305 mm) of the top and one permanent opening shall commence within 12 inches (305 mm) of the bottom of the enclosure. The minimum dimension of air openings shall be not less than 3 inches (76 mm).*

Discussion and Commentary: If the required volume of indoor combustion air is not available within the appliance enclosure, air may be pulled from adjoining interior spaces to satisfy the requirements. The code prescribes the minimum size and location of two openings—one high and one low—to communicate with other interior spaces. The free area of an opening describes the area without obstructions such as the solid portions of grilles or louvers. As with determining the minimum volume of indoor combustion air, the opening size is based on the total input rating of the appliances, provided each opening has at least 100 square inches of free area and a minimum dimension of at least 3 inches.

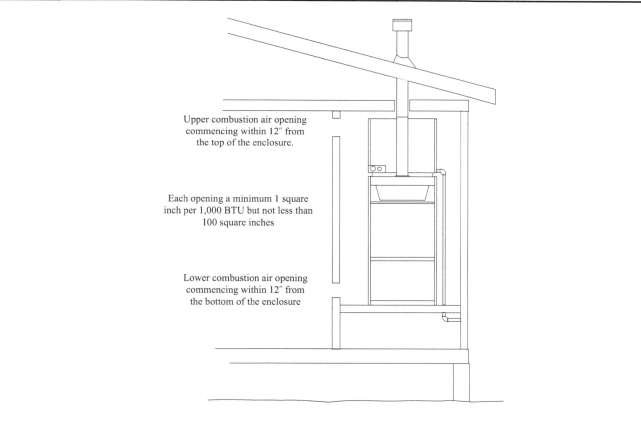

Indoor combustion air from space on same story

Placement of combustion air openings within 12 inches of the top and bottom of the enclosure ensures adequate air circulation between the enclosure and the other interior space.

Topic: Two Permanent Openings Method
Reference: IFGC 304.6.1
Category: General Regulations
Subject: Combustion, Ventilation and Dilution Air

Code Text: *Two permanent openings, one commencing within 12 inches (305 mm) of the top and one commencing within 12 inches (305 mm) of the bottom of the enclosure, shall be provided. The openings shall communicate directly, or by ducts, with the outdoors or spaces that freely communicate with the outdoors.* Net free area is based on the duct orientation and the total input rating of all appliances in the enclosure: (1) Direct or vertical ducts, 1 sq in. per 4,000 Btu/h; (2) Horizontal ducts, 1 sq in. per 2,000 Btu/h.

Discussion and Commentary: When adequate combustion air cannot be obtained from indoors, the code requires combustion air from outdoors. In addition to ducts and openings directly to the outdoors, attics and crawl spaces that freely communicate with the outdoors are approved locations for supplying outdoor combustion air. The provisions for the location and minimum free area of openings into the appliance enclosure are similar to the indoor combustion air requirements, with one opening placed near the ceiling and one opening near the floor of the enclosure to ensure adequate circulation of air.

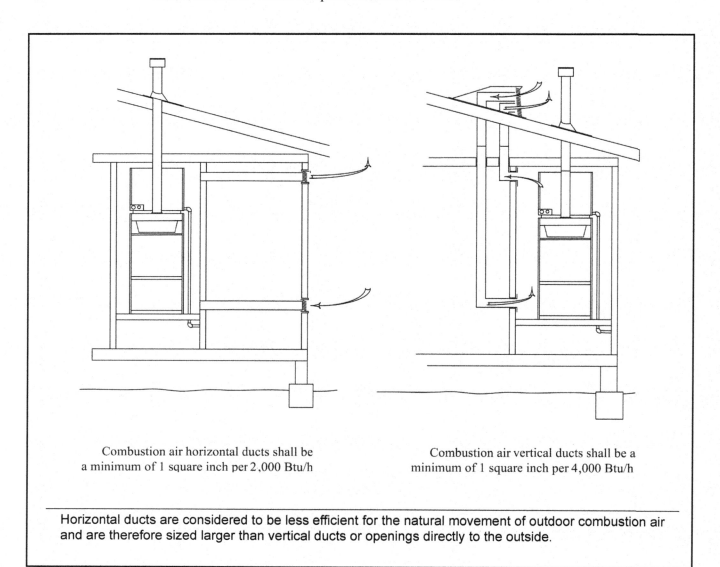

Combustion air horizontal ducts shall be a minimum of 1 square inch per 2,000 Btu/h

Combustion air vertical ducts shall be a minimum of 1 square inch per 4,000 Btu/h

Horizontal ducts are considered to be less efficient for the natural movement of outdoor combustion air and are therefore sized larger than vertical ducts or openings directly to the outside.

Topic: One Permanent Opening Method
Reference: IFGC 304.6.2
Category: General Regulations
Subject: Combustion, Ventilation and Dilution Air

Code Text: *One permanent opening, commencing within 12 inches (305 mm) of the top of the enclosure, shall be provided. The appliance shall have clearances of at least 1 inch (25 mm) from the sides and back and 6 inches (152 mm) from the front of the appliance. The opening shall directly communicate with the outdoors or through a vertical or horizontal duct to the outdoors, or spaces that freely communicate with the outdoors (see Figure 304.6.2) and shall have a minimum free area of 1 square inch per 3,000 Btu/h (734 mm^2/kW) of the total input rating of all appliances located in the enclosure and not less than the sum of the areas of all vent connectors in the space.*

Discussion and Commentary: As an alternative to the two-opening method for obtaining outdoor combustion air, the code permits a single opening within 12 inches of the top of the appliance enclosure when the opening and duct have a minimum free area of 1 square inch per 3,000 Btu/h of the total input rating of all appliances. This is a slightly larger opening size than is required for the vertical ducts or direct openings of the two-opening method. When the prescribed minimum clearances are provided around the appliances, testing has demonstrated that this design with a single opening provides adequate combustion air for safe operation of gas-fired appliances and is considered equivalent to the two-opening method.

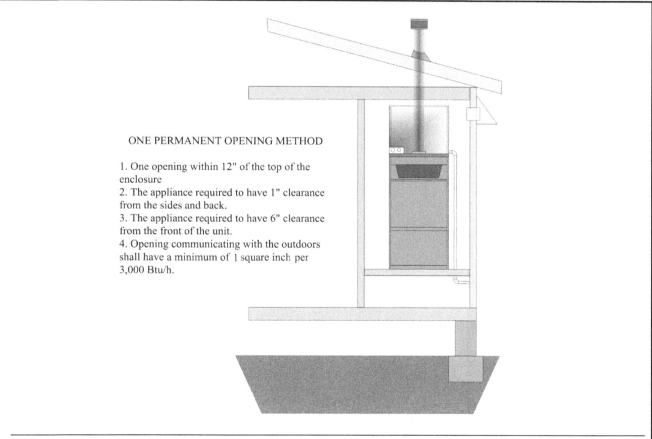

ONE PERMANENT OPENING METHOD

1. One opening within 12" of the top of the enclosure
2. The appliance required to have 1" clearance from the sides and back.
3. The appliance required to have 6" clearance from the front of the unit.
4. Opening communicating with the outdoors shall have a minimum of 1 square inch per 3,000 Btu/h.

To ensure an adequate supply of combustion air, the size of the opening or duct for the single-opening method must provide a minimum free area of 1 square inch per 3,000 Btu/h of the total input rating of all appliances and not less than the sum of all of the appliance connectors in the enclosure.

Topic: Combustion Air Ducts
Reference: IFGC 304.11

Category: General Regulations
Subject: Combustion, Ventilation and Dilution Air

Code Text: *Combustion air ducts shall comply with all of the following:*

1. *Ducts shall be constructed of galvanized steel complying with Chapter 6 of the* International Mechanical Code *or of a material having equivalent corrosion resistance, strength and rigidity.*

See the seven additional items listed in this section related to the construction, location and installation of combustion air ducts.

Discussion and Commentary: The IFGC references Chapter 6 of the *International Mechanical Code* (IMC), which regulates the construction and installation of air ducts, including provisions for seams, connections and supports. The IMC, in turn, references the *SMACNA HVAC Duct Construction Standards* for the construction of metal ducts. Generally, combustion air ducts are constructed of galvanized steel complying with the SMACNA standard. However, the code permits any duct material with equivalent performance characteristics.

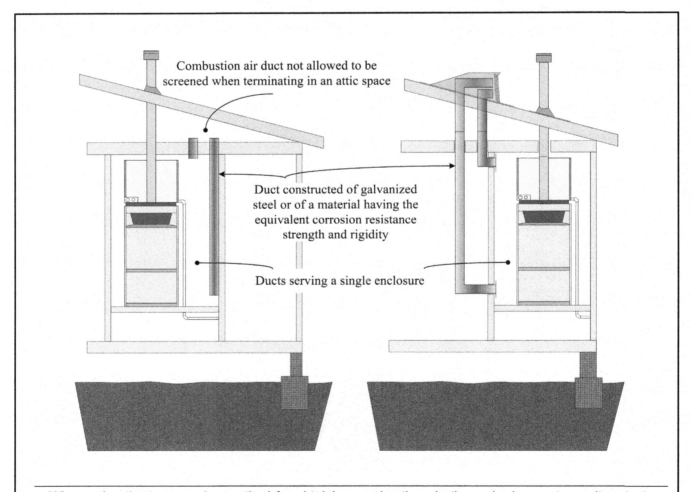

When using the two-opening method for obtaining combustion air, the code does not permit a single duct to serve both the upper and lower combustion air openings into the appliance enclosure. Separate ducts are required from the source of the combustion air to the appliance space.

Quiz

Study Session 2
IFGC Sections 301 through 304

1. Unless otherwise approved in accordance with Section 105, appliances regulated by this code shall be _____.

    a. certified
    b. listed
    c. vented
    d. evaluated

    Reference _____

2. Unlisted appliances _____.

    a. are not allowed to be installed
    b. require testing conducted by the manufacturer
    c. may be approved based upon an approved engineering evaluation
    d. are permitted to be installed in accordance with the manufacturer's installation instructions

    Reference _____

3. For a label affixed to a listed fuel gas appliance, which of the following is not required information?

    a. The appliance Btu/hour rating
    b. If the appliance is rated for 120 or 220 volt alternating current
    c. The approved fuel
    d. The minimum required clearances

    Reference _____

4. Combustion air requirements for appliances with power burners are determined by _____.
   a. the known air infiltration rate method
   b. engineering calculations
   c. research reports
   d. the manufacturer's instructions

   Reference _____

5. Conversion of an appliance to a different fuel gas is allowed if in accordance with the _____ instructions.
   a. engineer's
   b. inspector's
   c. manufacturer's
   d. contractor's

   Reference _____

6. Appliances in structures located in flood hazard areas shall be located at or above the _____.
   a. high water level
   b. elevation required by the IBC
   c. freeboard
   d. 100-year flood level

   Reference _____

7. Notching at the ends of wood joists shall not exceed _____ the joist depth.
   a. $1/2$
   b. $1/8$
   c. $3/8$
   d. $1/4$

   Reference _____

8. Cuts, notches and bored holes are prohibited in trusses except where _____.
   a. limited in size, number and location
   b. located in nonbearing members
   c. approved by the building inspector
   d. the effects are specifically considered in the design

   Reference _____

9. In bearing partitions, any wood stud is permitted to be cut or notched to a depth not exceeding_____ percent of its width.

   a. 25   b. 50
   c. 40   d. 10

   Reference _____

10. Notches in the flange of a cold-formed steel stud in a bearing wall _____.

    a. must be at least 16 inches from the bearing end
    b. cannot exceed 3 inches in length
    c. must be spaced at least 24 inches
    d. are not allowed

    Reference _____

11. When installed in a bedroom, a single wall-mounted unvented room heater is limited to an input rating not greater than _____ Btu/h.

    a. 5,000   b. 6,000
    c. 8,000   d. 10,000

    Reference _____

12. Appliances shall not be installed in a location subject to vehicle damage except _____.

    a. when listed for that particular installation
    b. when installed per the manufacturer's installation instructions
    c. where protected by an approved means
    d. when installed behind steel barriers

    Reference _____

13. Where used, draft hoods and draft barometric regulators shall be installed _____.

    a. on the roof of the building
    b. in a room adjacent to the appliances
    c. at the appliance vent connection
    d. in the same room as the appliance

    Reference _____

14. Where mechanical exhaust interferes with the operation of an appliance, _____ is required.

    a. an appliance enclosure

    b. makeup air

    c. an automatic appliance shut-off device

    d. an interlock between the appliance and exhaust fan

    Reference _____

15. Where the air-infiltration-rate is unknown, a room or space providing indoor combustion air requires a minimum volume of _____ cubic feet per 1,000 Btu/h of the appliance input rating.

    a. 15   b. 25

    c. 50   d. 75

    Reference _____

16. When using the known air-infiltration-rate method for indoor combustion air, the maximum infiltration rate that can be used in the equations is _____ ACH.

    a. 2.0   b. 1.0

    c. 0.75   d. 0.60

    Reference _____

17. Holes bored in solid wood joists shall be located not less than _____ inch(es) from the top and bottom joist.

    a. 2   b. 1 1/2

    c. 1   d. 1/2

    Reference _____

18. Openings obtaining indoor combustion air from a different story require a total minimum free area of _____ square inch(es) per 1,000 Btu/h of the total input rating of appliances.

    a. 2   b. 3

    c. 1   d. 4

    Reference _____

19. Where a space is provided outdoor combustion air through two openings, one opening must begin within _____ inches of the top and within _____ inches of the bottom of the enclosure.

    a. 3, 3   b. 6, 6
    c. 12, 12   d. 18, 18

    Reference_____

20. The minimum dimension of an outdoor combustion air opening is inches.

    a. 3   b. 8
    c. 6   d. 12

    Reference_____

21. Where a space is provided outdoor combustion air through a single opening, a clearance of at least _____ inches is required in front of the appliance.

    a. 6   b. 5
    c. 12   d. 10

    Reference_____

22. A mechanical combustion air system shall supply outdoor air at a rate not less than _____ cfm per 1,000 Btu/h of total input rating of all appliances located within the space.

    a. 15   b. 21
    c. 0.50   d. 0.35

    Reference_____

23. Where a screen is installed at a combustion air opening, the mesh size shall not be smaller than _____ inch.

    a. $1/8$ b. $1/2$
    c. $3/8$ d. $1/4$

    Reference_____

24. Galvanized steel ducts used for combustion air shall be constructed in accordance with the _____.

   a. *International Fuel Gas Code* (IFGC)

   b. *International Building Code* (IBC)

   c. *International Mechanical Code* (IMC)

   d. ACCA *Manual D*

   Reference_____

25. Within dwelling units, unobstructed _____ are permitted to convey combustion air.

   a. shafts   b. stud and joist spaces

   c. chases enclosing chimneys   d. chimneys

   Reference_____

Study Session

3

2021 IFGC Sections 305 through 310
General Regulations II

OBJECTIVE: To gain an understanding of the general code requirements governing the installation and location of equipment and appliances, access to appliances, electrical requirements, condensation provisions for high efficiency appliances and clearances to equipment.

REFERENCE: Sections 305 through 310, 2021 *International Fuel Gas Code*

KEY POINTS:
- Under what circumstances are appliance locations restricted?
- When are appliances required to have their ignition source located 18 inches above the floor?
- When is the ignition source of an appliance permitted to be located at the floor level in a hazardous location?
- When does the code require a boiler or furnace room to be separated from other occupancies?
- Appliances are required to be installed what distance above the adjoining grade level?
- What requirements apply to appliances serving repair garages?
- What are the access requirements to appliances and equipment installed in a room?
- What are the access requirements to appliances and equipment installed in attics?
- What are the access requirements to appliances and equipment installed in under-floor spaces?
- What code or standard governs the requirements for luminaires when an appliance is located in an attic or under floor space?
- Under what condition is an access ladder required?
- When is a working platform required for appliances located on roofs?
- When are guards required around a working platform when equipment is located on the roof of a building?
- What alternatives are allowed in place of a required guard?

KEY POINTS:
(Cont'd)
- Condensate piping serving condensing appliances shall be of what material?
- What is the minimum internal diameter for a condensate drain line?
- When are condensate drain lines required to be trapped?
- When are auxiliary drain pans required?
- When is a condensate pump required to shut down the appliance if the pump fails?
- When are reduced clearances permitted?
- Is gas piping permitted to be used as a grounding electrode?
- What are the bonding requirements for CSST gas piping?

Topic: Elevation of Ignition Source
Reference: IFGC 305.3

Category: General Regulations
Subject: Installation

Code Text: *Equipment and appliances having an ignition source shall be elevated such that the source of ignition is not less than 18 inches (457 mm) above the floor in hazardous locations and public garages, private garages, repair garages, motor fuel-dispensing facilities and parking garages. For the purpose of this section, rooms or spaces that are not part of the living space of a dwelling unit and that communicate directly with a private garage through openings shall be considered to be part of the private garage.* See the exception for appliances that are listed as flammable vapor ignition resistant.

Discussion and Commentary: By definition, an ignition source is a flame, spark or hot surface capable of igniting flammable vapors. Because flammable vapors are heavier than air and collect near the floor of a garage or hazardous location, the code requires any source of ignition that is part of an appliance to be elevated at least 18 inches above the floor. Note that the minimum elevation distance is measured to the lowest ignition source and not to the base of the appliance. Appliances that are listed as flammable vapor ignition resistant are designed to control the intake of combustion air and prevent the escape of any ignited vapors to outside the combustion chamber. With safeguards built in to the appliance, elevation of the ignition source is not necessary.

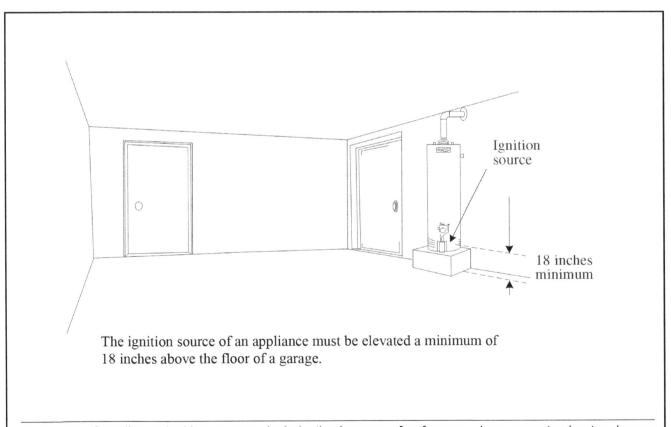

The ignition source of an appliance must be elevated a minimum of 18 inches above the floor of a garage.

Examples of appliance ignition sources include the burners of a furnace, dryer or water heater; burner igniters or electrical relays; switches; contacts; and electrical motors, which can create a spark.

Topic: Installation in Residential Garages
Reference: IFGC 305.3.1
Category: General Regulations
Subject: Installation

Code Text: *In residential garages where appliances are installed in a separate, enclosed space having access only from outside of the garage, such appliances shall be permitted to be installed at floor level, provided that the required combustion air is taken from the exterior of the garage.*

Discussion and Commentary: Appliances that are installed in residential garages and have an ignition source are permitted to be installed at floor level only if the appliance is in an enclosed space without any openings or access into the garage. Access to the appliance enclosure must be from outside the garage. Combustion air also must be obtained directly from the outside. This separation adequately isolates the ignition source from the garage area, and elevation of the appliance is not necessary.

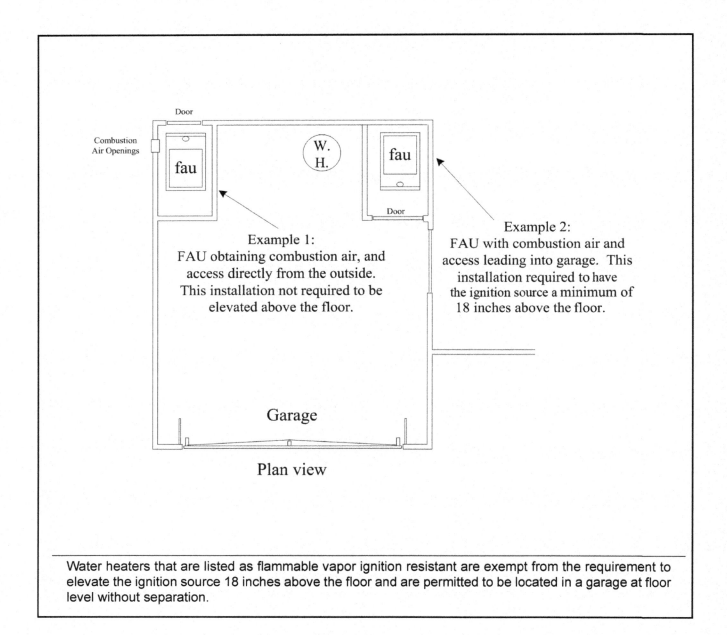

Water heaters that are listed as flammable vapor ignition resistant are exempt from the requirement to elevate the ignition source 18 inches above the floor and are permitted to be located in a garage at floor level without separation.

Topic: Clearances from Grade
Reference: IFGC 305.7

Category: General Regulations
Subject: Installation

Code Text: *Equipment and appliances installed at grade level shall be supported on a level concrete slab or other approved material extending not less than 3 inches (76 mm) above adjoining grade or shall be suspended not less than 6 inches (152 mm) above adjoining grade. Such supports shall be installed in accordance with the manufacturer's installation instructions.*

Discussion and Commentary: Appliances installed outdoors or underneath a building are subject to deterioration and corrosion when installed on soil or rocks. The IFGC requires equipment be elevated to provide safe operation and to prolong the life of the appliance. When supported by a level concrete slab on the ground, the appliance must maintain a clearance of at least 3 inches above grade. Equipment suspended underneath a building or supported by brackets on the side of a building requires a minimum clearance of 6 inches above the ground.

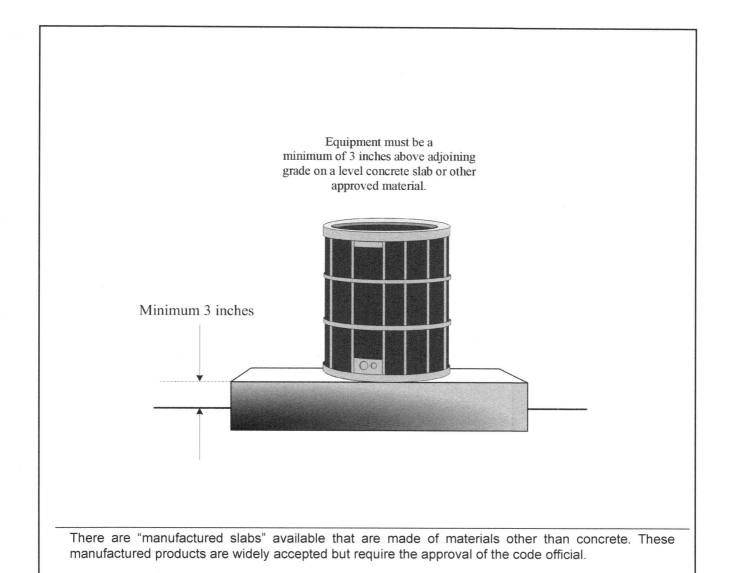

There are "manufactured slabs" available that are made of materials other than concrete. These manufactured products are widely accepted but require the approval of the code official.

Topic: Appliances in Rooms
Reference: IFGC 306.2

Category: General Regulations
Subject: Access and Service Space

Code Text: *Rooms containing appliances shall be provided with a door and an unobstructed passageway measuring not less than 36 inches (914 mm) wide and 80 inches (2032 mm) high.* An exception for dwelling units permits a door and passageway not less than 24 inches wide.

Discussion and Commentary: A door and passageway measuring 3 feet wide by 6 feet 8 inches provide adequate space to access an appliance for service and repair, and to remove or replace the appliance without removing permanent construction or other obstructions. Although this is a common size door in commercial applications, the code recognizes that dwelling units often have smaller spaces and appliances. A 24-inch wide access passageway is adequate to service residential appliances. The height of the passageway in this case need only be sufficient to remove the largest appliance. Note that a 30-inch deep level working space is required in front of the appliance, but this space may include the doorway with the door open, provided the working space has a height of not less than 30 inches.

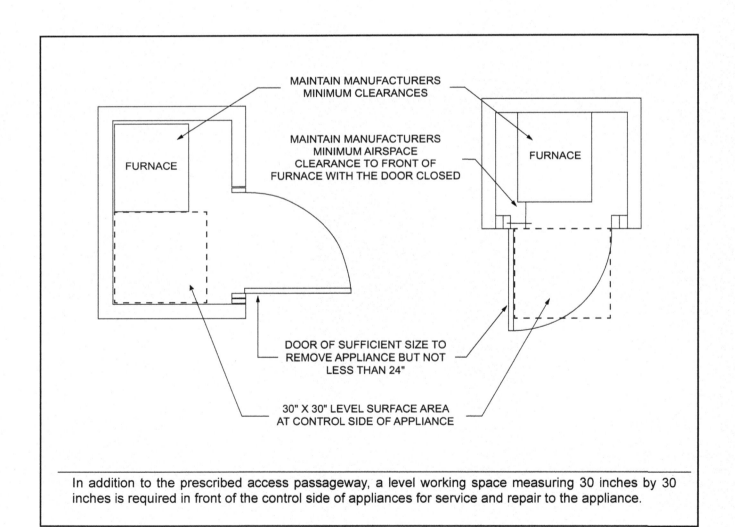

In addition to the prescribed access passageway, a level working space measuring 30 inches by 30 inches is required in front of the control side of appliances for service and repair to the appliance.

Topic: Appliances in Attics
Reference: IFGC 306.3

Category: General Regulations
Subject: Access and Service Spa

Code Text: *Attics containing appliances shall be provided with an opening and unobstructed passageway large enough to allow removal of the largest appliance. The passageway shall not be less than 30 inches (762 mm) high and 22 inches (559 mm) wide and not more than 20 feet (6096 mm) in length measured along the centerline of the passageway from the opening to the appliance. The passageway shall have continuous solid flooring not less than 24 inches (610 mm) wide. A level service space not less than 30 inches (762 mm) deep and 30 inches (762 mm) wide shall be present at the front or service side of the appliance. The clear access opening dimensions shall be a minimum of 20 inches by 30 inches (508 mm by 762 mm), and large enough to allow removal of the largest appliance. See the exceptions for 1) service permitted at the access opening and 2) increased length of passageway to 50 feet where 6-foot height is provided.*

Discussion and Commentary: Access to equipment in attics is required to permit inspection, service, maintenance or removal. The passageway allows for personnel to access equipment and exit safely. Typically, the installation of appliances in attics must be considered in the building design process. Not only is adequate space required, but the attic design must accommodate solid flooring for the passageway without obstructions such as truss web members, ducts or pipes. In addition, the design of structural members must account for the dead and live load of equipment, the passageway and service personnel.

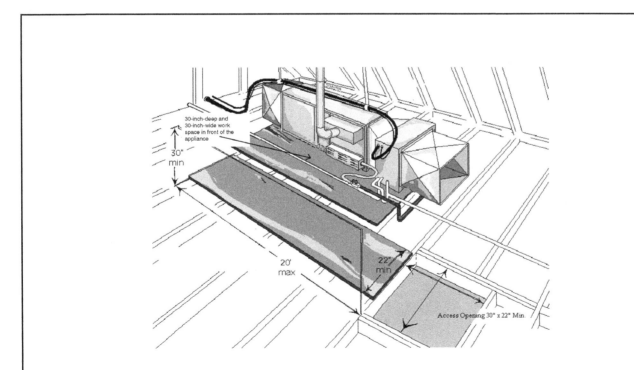

The listing for certain types of equipment may prohibit installation in attics.

Topic: Appliances under Floors
Reference: IFGC 306.4
Category: General Regulations
Subject: Access and Service Space

Code Text: *Under-floor spaces containing appliances shall be provided with an access opening and unobstructed passageway large enough to remove the largest appliance. The passageway shall not be less than 30 inches (762 mm) high and 22 inches (559 mm) wide, nor more than 20 feet (6096 mm) in length measured along the centerline of the passageway from the opening to the appliance. A level service space not less than 30 inches (762 mm) deep and 30 inches (762 mm) wide shall be present at the front or service side of the appliance. If the depth of the passageway or the service space exceeds 12 inches (305 mm) below the adjoining grade, the walls of the passageway shall be lined with concrete or masonry extending 4 inches (102 mm) above the adjoining grade and having sufficient lateral-bearing capacity to resist collapse. The clear access opening dimensions shall be a minimum of 22 inches by 30 inches (559 mm by 762 mm), and large enough to allow removal of the largest appliance.* See the exceptions fork: (1) service permitted at the access opening, and (2) unlimited length of passageway where height of 6 feet is provided.

Discussion and Commentary: Appliances are often installed in attics or under-floor spaces (crawl spaces) in order to better utilize the building's finished floor area. However, it is important to provide access to equipment in these limited-space areas to allow for inspection, service, maintenance and removal of the appliances. Similar to the attic access provisions, appliance installations in under-floor spaces require an unobstructed passageway that is limited to 20 feet in length when the height is at least 30 inches. Although the length of the passageway is unlimited if the ceiling height is at least 6 feet, crawl spaces typically have headroom that is less than 6 feet. As with attics, the code permits the service and removal of an appliance through the access opening without the need for a passageway or a 30-inch by 30-inch level working space.

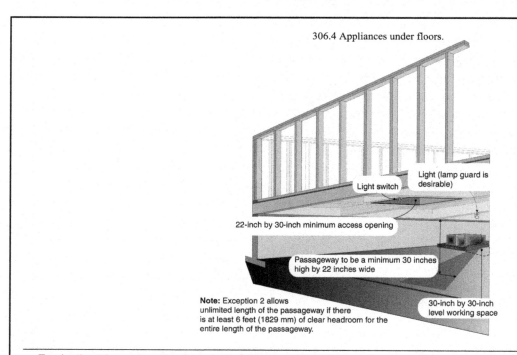

306.4 Appliances under floors.

For both attic and under floor installations, a light fixture (luminaire) and a receptacle outlet are required at the appliance location for use during the service or repair of the equipment. The switch controlling the light fixture must be located at the entry to the passageway.

Topic: Equipment on Roofs
Reference: IFGC 306.5
Category: General Regulations
Subject: Access and Service Space

Code Text: *Where equipment requiring access or appliances are located on an elevated structure or the roof of a building such that personnel will have to climb higher than 16 feet above grade to access such equipment or appliances, an interior or exterior means of access shall be provided. Such access shall not require climbing over obstructions greater than 30 inches (762 mm) in height or walking on roofs having a slope greater than 4 units vertical in 12 units horizontal (33-percent slope). Such access shall not require the use of portable ladders.*

Discussion and Commentary: Portable ladders are permitted for access to equipment located on the roof of buildings or on elevated structures when the equipment is located not more than 16 feet above the grade or floor below. For equipment and appliances located over 16 feet in height, a permanent fixed ladder attached to the building or some other approved permanent means of access is required. The height is measured from the grade or floor to the level service space of the appliance. The height of a parapet is included in the measurement.

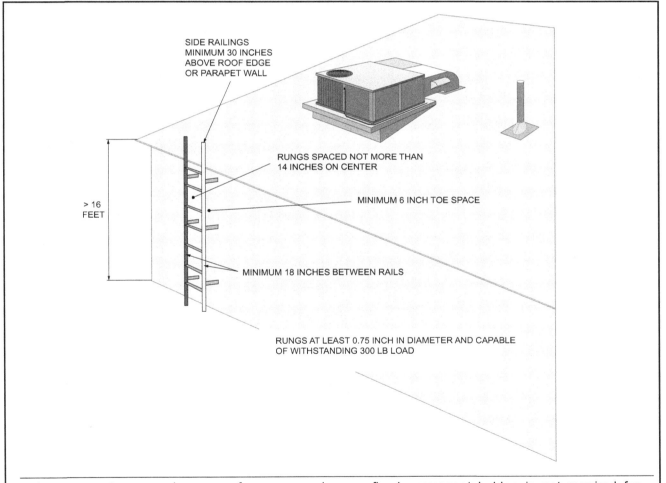

A permanent approved means of access, such as a fixed permanent ladder, is not required for installations of Group R-3 occupancies.

Topic: Permanent Ladders for Roof Access **Category:** General Regulations
Reference: IFGC 306.5 **Subject:** Access and Service Space

Code Text: *Permanent ladders installed to provide the required access shall comply with the following minimum design criteria:* The list includes (1) side railing extension of 30 inches, (2) maximum rung spacing of 14 inches, (3) minimum toe spacing 6 inches deep, (4) minimum 18 inches between rails, (5) minimum rung diameter of 0.75-inch with 300-pound load capacity, (6) landings for ladders over 30 feet in height, (7) climbing clearance of 30 inches perpendicular to rungs, (8) bottom landing of 30 inches by 30 inches, (9) corrosion protection, and (10) access required.

Discussion and Commentary: A permanent ladder is one method to satisfy the approved means of access requirements for equipment or appliances installed more than 16 feet above the ground or floor surface. The code includes specific design criteria and dimensions that were developed from OSHA regulations. In addition to width, rung and toe space dimension requirements, ladder side rails are required to extend above the parapet or roof surface at least 30 inches to provide a safe transition from the ladder to the roof for service personnel.

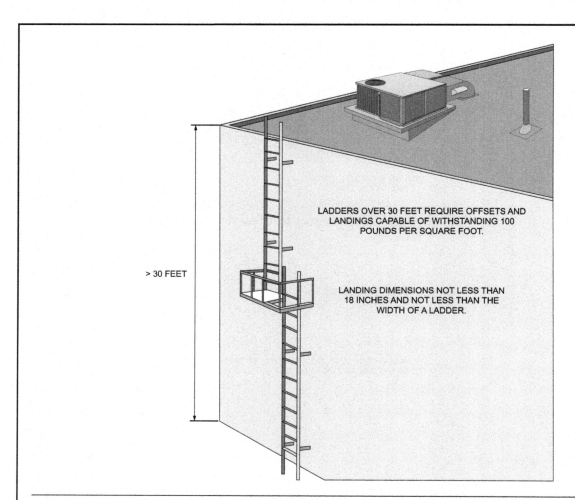

Fixed permanent ladders more than 30 feet in height have additional requirements including offset sections and landings with guards. The landings must be designed to support a load of 100 pounds per square foot and have minimum dimensions not less than 18 inches.

Topic: Sloped Roofs
Reference: IFGC 306.5.1

Category: General Regulations
Subject: Access and Service Space

Code Text: *Where appliances, equipment, fans or other components that require service are installed on a roof having a slope of 3 units vertical in 12 units horizontal (25-percent slope) or greater and having an edge more than 30 inches (762 mm) above grade at such edge, a level platform shall be provided on each side of the appliance or equipment to which access is required for service, repair or maintenance. The platform shall be not less than 30 inches (762 mm) in any dimension and shall be provided with guards. The guards shall extend not less than 42 inches (1067 mm) above the platform, shall be constructed so as to prevent the passage of a 21-inch-diameter (533 mm) sphere and shall comply with the loading requirements for guards specified in the* International Building Code. *Access shall not require walking on roofs having a slope greater than 4 units vertical in 12 units horizontal (33-percent slope).*

Discussion and Commentary: Sloped roofs present a challenge for maintenance and service personnel in both traveling to an appliance and in performing work with their tools at the appliance location. Low-slope roofs with a pitch of less than 3:12 are considered sufficiently flat to provide a safe walking and working surface. A roof with a slope of at least 3:12 and not more than 4:12 is fairly easy to walk across without toe holds or safety devices, but these slopes do require a level working surface at the appliance for safety of personnel and a means to prevent tools from sliding. The level work platform requires a 42-inch high guard to prevent workers from stepping off the platform and possibly falling off of the roof. Roof slopes greater than 4:12 are not considered to provide a reasonable level of safety for service personnel traveling to an appliance location, and another means of access is required in this case.

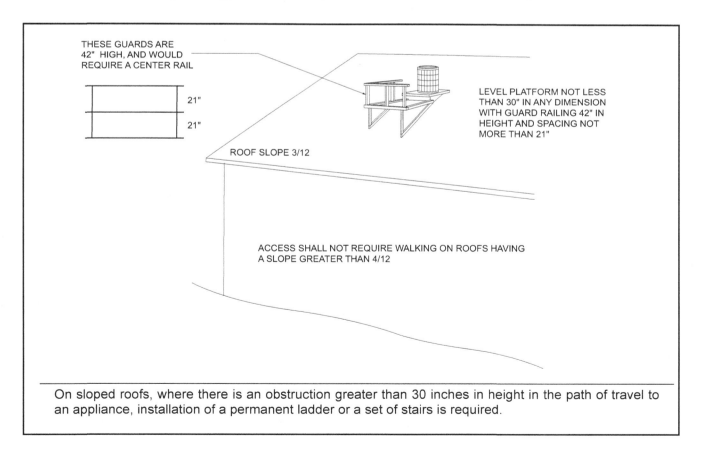

On sloped roofs, where there is an obstruction greater than 30 inches in height in the path of travel to an appliance, installation of a permanent ladder or a set of stairs is required.

Topic: Auxiliary Drain Pan
Reference: IFGC 307.5
Category: General Regulations
Subject: Condensate Disposal

Code Text: *Category IV condensing appliances shall be provided with an auxiliary drain pan where damage to any building component will occur as a result of stoppage in the condensate drainage system. Such pan shall be installed in accordance with the applicable provisions of Section 307 of the* International Mechanical Code. ***Exception:*** *An auxiliary drain pan shall not be required for appliances that automatically shut down operation in the event of a stoppage in the condensate drainage system.*

Discussion and Commentary: Condensate typically is produced by evaporators and cooling coils regulated by the *International Mechanical Code* (IMC), but low temperature flue gases of Category IV gas-fired appliances also produce condensate and are regulated by the IFGC. Installation of condensate drain lines are required to also comply with the *International Plumbing Code* (IPC). Primary drain lines must slope toward the point of termination and terminate in an approved location. When a condensing appliance is installed in a location, such as an attic or a space with a story below, where condensate leakage will cause damage to building components, an auxiliary drain pan is required to be installed below the appliance. The applicable installation requirements and dimensions for the drain pan are found in the *International Mechanical Code*.

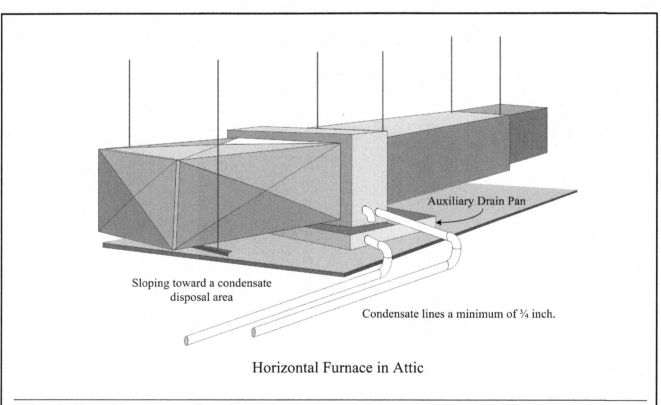

Horizontal Furnace in Attic

As an alternative to the auxiliary drain pan requirement, it is acceptable to install an approved device that automatically shuts down the appliance if a blockage occurs in the primary condensate line.

Topic: Condensate Pumps	**Category:** General Regulations
Reference: IFGC 307.6	**Subject:** Condensate Disposal

Code Text: *Condensate pumps located in uninhabitable spaces, such as attics and crawl spaces, shall be connected to the appliance or equipment served such that when the pump fails, the appliance or equipment will be prevented from operating. Pumps shall be installed in accordance with the manufacturer's instructions.*

Discussion and Commentary: Condensate pumps are often located in attics and crawl spaces and above ceilings where they are not readily observable. If they fail, the condensate overflow can cause damage to building elements. The majority of such pumps are equipped with simple float controls that can be wired in series with the appliance control circuit. When the pump system fails, the float rises in the reservoir and opens a switch, shutting down the appliance before the condensate starts to overflow the reservoir. The IFGC requires condensate pumps installed in uninhabitable spaces to have this feature and be connected to the appliance or equipment to prevent overflow.

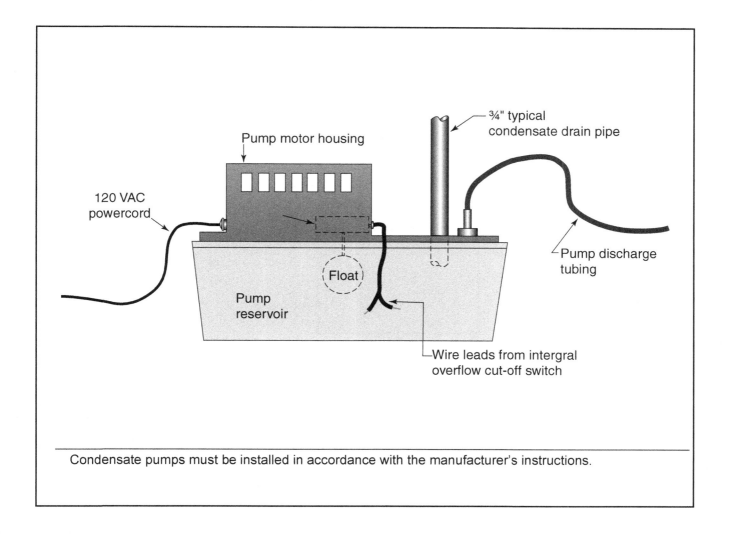

Condensate pumps must be installed in accordance with the manufacturer's instructions.

Topic: Reduction Table

Category: General Regulations

Reference: IFGC 308.2

Subject: Clearance Reduction

Code Text: *The allowable clearance reduction shall be based on one of the methods specified in Table 308.2 or shall utilize a reduced clearance protective assembly listed and labeled in accordance with UL 1618. Where required clearances are not listed in Table 308.2, the reduced clearances shall be determined by linear interpolation between the distances listed in the table. Reduced clearances shall not be derived by extrapolation below the range of the table. The reduction of the required clearances to combustibles for listed and labeled appliances and equipment shall be in accordance with the requirements of this section except that such clearances shall not be reduced where reduction is specifically prohibited by the terms of the appliance or equipment listing [see Figures 308.2(1) through 308.2(3)].*

Discussion and Commentary: Appliances listed for certain clearances from combustible construction may have those clearances reduced in accordance with Table 308.2. Most of the methods listed in Table 308.2 utilize the movement of air through convection as part of the protection of the building components. In some cases, the listing of certain appliances may not allow a reduction of the prescribed clearances, and this information is reflected in the manufacturer's installation instructions. Maintaining the clear air space behind and around the edges of the heat shield is critical to this convective cooling process to prevent the ignition of combustible materials.

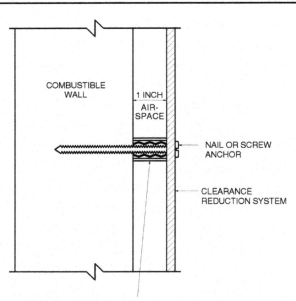

1-INCH NONCOMBUSTIBLE SPACER SUCH AS STACKED WASHERS, SMALL-DIAMETER PIPE, TUBING OR ELECTRICAL CONDUIT.

MASONRY WALLS CAN BE ATTACHED TO COMBUSTIBLE WALLS USING WALL TIES.

DO NOT USE SPACERS DIRECTLY BEHIND APPLIANCE OR CONNECTOR.

Wall protector clearance reduction system

Regardless of the type of protective assembly installed, a minimum 1-inch air space is always required between the appliance and clearance reduction system. For those systems utilizing an air space, a minimum 1-inch air gap between the clearance reduction system and combustible construction is required.

Topic: CSST
Reference: IFGC 310.2
Category: General Regulations
Subject: Electrical Bonding

Code Text: *This section applies to corrugated stainless steel tubing (CSST) that is not listed with an arc-resistant jacket or coating system in accordance with ANSI LC 1/CSA 6.26. CSST gas piping systems and piping systems containing one or more segments of CSST shall be electrically continuous and bonded to the electrical service grounding electrode system or, where provided, the lightning protection grounding electrode system.*

Discussion and Commentary: Electrical bonding of corrugated stainless steel tubing (CSST) to the building's grounding electrode system provides a fault path to ground and protects the gas tubing against perforation due to lightning-induced current surges. The bonding jumper must be 6 AWG or larger copper wire and connect to a CSST fitting or to metal gas pipe or fitting. Connections must be accomplished with approved clamps or devices listed for the application in accordance with NFPA 70, *National Electrical Code* (NEC).

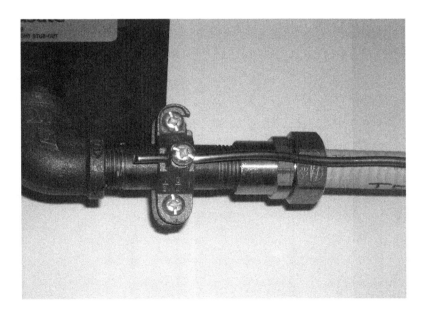

To maintain its effectiveness, the bonding jumper from the gas piping to the grounding electrode system is limited to 75 feet in length. This bonding jumper is not required for listed arc-resistant CSST that is connected to an appliance provided with an equipment grounding conductor.

Quiz

Study Session 3
IFGC Sections 305 through 310

1. Equipment and appliances having an ignition source shall _____ in Group H Occupancies or control areas where open use, handling or dispensing of combustible, flammable or explosive materials occurs.

    a. not be installed

    b. be elevated

    c. be listed as flammable ignition resistant

    d. be isolated in a separate room

    Reference_____

2. Appliances having an ignition sources shall be elevated such that the ignition source is not less than _____ inches above the floor in a private garage.

    a. 12   b. 18

    c. 6   d. 30

    Reference_____

3. Where vehicles are capable of passing under an appliance installed in a public garage, the appliance shall be installed a minimum of _____ inches higher than the tallest vehicle garage door opening.

    a. 24   b. 18

    c. 12   d. 6

    Reference_____

4. Unless otherwise protected from impact, appliances located in a public garage shall be installed a minimum of _____ feet above the floor.

    a. 12   b. 15

    c. 10   d. 8

    Reference_____

5. Unless otherwise protected from impact, appliances located in a private garage shall be installed a minimum of _____ feet above the floor.

    a. 12   b. 10

    c. 8   d. 6

    Reference_____

6. Where the opening dimensions are large enough to allow removal of the largest pieces of equipment installed in an under-floor space, the clear access opening to the under-floor area shall be a minimum of _____.

    a. 18 inches by 24 inches   b. 22 inches by 24 inches

    c. 22 inches by 30 inches   d. 30 inches by 30 inches

    Reference_____

7. Guards are not required for rooftop appliances requiring service where _____.

    a. approved fall-restraint devices are installed

    b. the appliance is at least 8 feet from the roof edge

    c. the roof slope is less than 3/12

    d. the roof edge is not greater than 10 feet above grade

    Reference_____

8. Suspended mechanical equipment shall be installed a minimum of _____ inches above the adjoining grade.

    a. 3   b. 6

    c. 8   d. 12

    Reference_____

9. Unless located within a dwelling unit, rooms containing appliances shall be provided with a door and an unobstructed passageway measuring not less than _____ inches wide and 80 inches high.

    a. 24
    b. 32
    c. 36
    d. 30

    Reference_____

10. Appliances located in an attic shall be provided with a level service space not less than _____ inches deep and _____ inches wide.

    a. 30, 24
    b. 24, 30
    c. 30, 30
    d. 30, 36

    Reference_____

11. A 30-inch high attic passageway serving a gas appliance is limited in length to no more than _____ feet.

    a. 20
    b. 18
    c. 12
    d. 24

    Reference_____

12. Where an appliance is located in an attic, a _____ is required at the access opening to the attic passageway.

    a. luminaire
    b. receptacle outlet
    c. level work surface
    d. light switch

    Reference_____

13. A permanent approved means of access is required for appliances installed on roofs at a height exceeding _____ feet.

    a. 10
    b. 16
    c. 20
    d. 24

    Reference_____

14. Required guards installed around rooftop service platforms shall be not less than _____ inches in height.

    a. 30 b. 36
    c. 42 d. 48

    Reference_____

15. Where approved roof-mounted fall-restraint devices are installed in place of a required guard, the devices must be installed every _____ feet or less along the ridge line.

    a. 10 b. 15
    c. 20 d. 25

    Reference_____

16. Catwalks installed to provide the required access to rooftop equipment shall be a minimum of _____ inches wide.

    a. 36 b. 30
    c. 24 d. 18

    Reference_____

17. Condensate waste and drain lines shall be not less than _____ -inch internal diameter.

    a. 1   b. $^1/_2$
    c. $^5/_8$ d. $^3/_4$

    Reference_____

18. Condensate piping for fuel burning condensing appliances shall maintain a minimum horizontal slope of _____ units vertical in 12 units horizontal.

    a. $^1/_8$ b. $^1/_4$
    c. $^3/_8$ d. $^1/_2$

    Reference_____

19. An automatic appliance shut-off device is required for condensate pumps located _____.

   a. in a basement
   b. in an attic
   c. in a mechanical room
   d. more than 10 feet from the condensing appliance

   Reference_____

20. Where appliances are supported by a concrete slab, the slab shall extend at least _____ inches above the adjoining grade.

   a. 3
   b. 4
   c. 6
   d. 9

   Reference_____

21. Where a reduction in clearance to combustible materials is permitted, the side clearance for an appliance is permitted to be reduced from 12 inches to a minimum of _____ inches by installing No. 24 gage galvanized sheet metal with a ventilated air space.

   a. 6
   b. 9
   c. 3
   d. 4

   Reference_____

22. For a clearance reduction system using ventilated air space, the system shall maintain an air space clearance to combustible materials of at least _____ inch(es).

   a. $^1/_2$
   b. $1\,^1/_2$
   c. 1
   d. 2

   Reference_____

23. Reduced clearance protective assemblies for gas appliances shall be placed a minimum of _____ inch(es) from the appliance.

   a. $^1/_2$
   b. $1\,^1/_2$
   c. 1
   d. 2

   Reference_____

24. The bonding jumper used to bond corrugated stainless steel tubing (CSST) gas piping to the grounding system shall be not smaller than _____ AWG copper wire or equivalent.

    a. 12
    b. 10
    c. 8
    d. 6

    Reference_____

25. The maximum length of an electrical bonding jumper for a corrugated stainless steel tubing (CSST) system is _____ feet.

    a. 150
    b. 25
    c. 100
    d. 75

    Reference_____

Study Session

2021 IFGC Sections 401 through 406
Gas Piping Installations I

OBJECTIVE: To gain an understanding of the construction, location, installation and testing of the fuel-gas distribution system.

REFERENCE: Sections 401 through 406, 2021 *International Fuel Gas Code*

KEY POINTS:
- What are the requirements for identifying exposed gas piping?
- What type of identification is required for multiple gas meters?
- How are gas piping systems sized to meet the minimum demand for appliances?
- What tables are permitted to be used for gas pipe sizing?
- What are the recognized methods for sizing gas piping?
- What are the requirements for sizing gas piping using the branch length method?
- What materials are permitted for gas piping?
- What is the maximum content of hydrogen sulfide allowed in the gas if copper or copper alloy pipes are used?
- What are the requirements for anodeless risers?
- What are the design considerations for selecting the appropriate piping joints and fittings?
- Gas piping installations shall be prohibited under what conditions?
- When is gas piping permitted to be installed in solid walls?
- What requirements apply to a gas line penetrating a foundation wall?
- What are the requirements for installing gas piping in a solid floor?
- Does a conduit that houses a gas line and terminates to the outside have to be sealed?
- At what depth shall underground gas piping be buried?
- What are the requirements for installing underground gas piping beneath a building?
- What are the requirements for terminating underground gas piping inside a building?

KEY POINTS:
(Cont'd)

- What is the minimum required distance that the unthreaded portion of a gas piping outlet must extend when penetrating a finished floor, ceiling or wall?
- Plastic piping installations are subject to what limitations when installed outdoors?
- What testing procedures are required when a gas piping system is pressurized?
- What fittings are permitted in concealed locations?
- When does gas piping require protection against penetration by fasteners?
- What medium is permitted for pressure testing of a gas piping system?
- What test pressures must be used when testing a gas piping system?
- What is the minimum required duration of the test for a gas piping system?
- What methods are permitted for checking a leak in a gas piping system?
- When does the code require a gas piping system to be checked for leakage?
- What purging procedures are required before gas pipes are put into service?

Topic: Identification	Category: Gas Piping Installations
Reference: IFGC 401.5	Subject: General Requirements

Code Text: *For other than steel pipe and CSST, exposed piping shall be identified by a yellow label marked "Gas" in black letters. The marking shall be spaced at intervals not exceeding 5 feet (1524 mm). The marking shall not be required on pipe located in the same room as the appliance served. CSST shall be identified as required by ANSI LC 1/CSA 6.26.*

Discussion and Commentary: Identification of gas piping provides a safeguard against inadvertent cutting, disassembling or modifying of piping containing pressurized fuel gas, any of which could cause serious injury to people or damage to the building. Appropriate labels prevent gas piping from being mistaken for plumbing, heating, cooling, compressed air or process piping. This is particularly important when copper tubing or piping is used for gas piping because these materials are often utilized in plumbing systems or for carrying other fluids or gases. Gas piping connected to an appliance and located in the same room as the appliance does not require further identification, because the use of the piping is readily apparent.

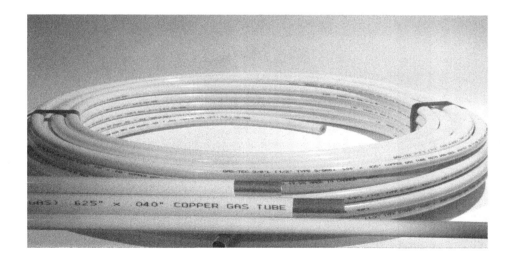

Steel piping is exempt from the identification requirement because it is the traditional gas pipe material and recognized as such.

Topic: Piping Meter Identification
Reference: IFGC 401.7
Category: Gas Piping Installations
Subject: General Requirements

Code Text: *Piping from multiple meter installations shall be marked with an approved permanent identification by the installer so that the piping system supplied by each meter is readily identifiable.*

Discussion and Commentary: Identification at the meter location allows a service and emergency personnel to readily locate the meter and shut off valve serving that particular piping system.

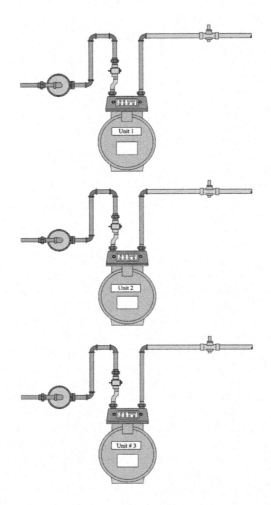

Piping from multiple meters shall be marked with an approved permanent identification

Where there are multiple meters, identification of the piping system at the meter also prevents interconnection between systems and between spaces.

Topic: Sizing
Reference: IFGC 402.3
Category: Gas Piping Installations
Subject: Pipe Sizing

Code Text: *Gas piping shall be sized in accordance with one of the following: (1) Pipe sizing tables or sizing equations in accordance with Section 402.4 or 402.5 as applicable, (2) The sizing tables included in a listed piping system's manufacturer's installation instructions, (3) Engineering methods.*

Discussion and Commentary: Sizing gas piping using Table 402.4(1) is generally easier than other methods. The table is based on traditional steel pipe size designation as used in the material standards. A total of 37 sizing tables are included in the IFGC for various gas piping materials, pressures and fuels.

TABLE 402.4(1) SCHEDULE 40 METALLIC PIPE

Gas	Natural
Inlet Pressure	Less than 2 psi
Pressure Drop	0.3 in. w.c.
Specific Gravity	0.60

	PIPE SIZE (inch)												
Nominal	1/2	3/4	1	1 1/4	1 1/2	2	2 1/2	3	4	5	6	8	10	12
Actual ID	0.622	0.824	1.049	1.380	1.610	2.067	2.469	3.068	4.026	5.047	6.065	7.981	10.020	11.938
Length (ft)	Capacity in Cubic Feet of Gas Per Hour													
10	131	273	514	1,060	1,580	3,050	4,860	8,580	17,500	31,700	51,300	105,000	191,000	303,000
20	90	188	353	726	1,090	2,090	3,340	5,900	12,000	21,800	35,300	72,400	132,000	208,000
30	72	151	284	583	873	1,680	2,680	4,740	9,660	17,500	28,300	58,200	106,000	167,000
40	62	129	243	499	747	1,440	2,290	4,050	8,270	15,000	24,200	49,800	90,400	143,000
50	55	114	215	442	662	1,280	2,030	3,590	7,330	13,300	21,500	44,100	80,100	127,000
60	50	104	195	400	600	1,160	1,840	3,260	6,640	12,000	19,500	40,000	72,600	115,000
70	46	95	179	368	552	1,060	1,690	3,000	6,110	11,100	17,900	36,800	66,800	106,000
80	42	89	167	343	514	989	1,580	2,790	5,680	10,300	16,700	34,200	62,100	98,400
90	40	83	157	322	482	928	1,480	2,610	5,330	9,650	15,600	32,100	58,300	92,300
100	38	79	148	304	455	877	1,400	2,470	5,040	9,110	14,800	30,300	55,100	87,200
125	33	70	131	269	403	777	1,240	2,190	4,460	8,080	13,100	26,900	48,800	77,300
150	30	63	119	244	366	704	1,120	1,980	4,050	7,320	11,900	24,300	44,200	70,000
175	28	58	109	224	336	648	1,030	1,820	3,720	6,730	10,900	22,400	40,700	64,400
200	26	54	102	209	313	602	960	1,700	3,460	6,260	10,100	20,800	37,900	59,900
250	23	48	90	185	277	534	851	1,500	3,070	5,550	8,990	18,500	33,500	53,100
300	21	43	82	168	251	484	771	1,360	2,780	5,030	8,150	16,700	30,400	48,100
350	19	40	75	154	231	445	709	1,250	2,560	4,630	7,490	15,400	28,000	44,300
400	18	37	70	143	215	414	660	1,170	2,380	4,310	6,970	14,300	26,000	41,200
450	17	35	66	135	202	389	619	1,090	2,230	4,040	6,540	13,400	24,400	38,600
500	16	33	62	127	191	367	585	1,030	2,110	3,820	6,180	12,700	23,100	36,500
550	15	31	59	121	181	349	556	982	2,000	3,620	5,870	12,100	21,900	34,700
600	14	30	56	115	173	333	530	937	1,910	3,460	5,600	11,500	20,900	33,100
650	14	29	54	110	165	318	508	897	1,830	3,310	5,360	11,000	20,000	31,700
700	13	27	52	106	159	306	488	862	1,760	3,180	5,150	10,600	19,200	30,400
750	13	26	50	102	153	295	470	830	1,690	3,060	4,960	10,200	18,500	29,300
800	12	26	48	99	148	285	454	802	1,640	2,960	4,790	9,840	17,900	28,300
850	12	25	46	95	143	275	439	776	1,580	2,860	4,640	9,530	17,300	27,400
900	11	24	45	93	139	267	426	752	1,530	2,780	4,500	9,240	16,800	26,600
950	11	23	44	90	135	259	413	731	1,490	2,700	4,370	8,970	16,300	25,800
1,000	11	23	43	87	131	252	402	711	1,450	2,620	4,250	8,720	15,800	25,100
1,100	10	21	40	83	124	240	382	675	1,380	2,490	4,030	8,290	15,100	23,800
1,200	NA	20	39	79	119	229	364	644	1,310	2,380	3,850	7,910	14,400	22,700
1,300	NA	20	37	76	114	219	349	617	1,260	2,280	3,680	7,570	13,700	21,800
1,400	NA	19	35	73	109	210	335	592	1,210	2,190	3,540	7,270	13,200	20,900
1,500	NA	18	34	70	105	203	323	571	1,160	2,110	3,410	7,010	12,700	20,100
1,600	NA	18	33	68	102	196	312	551	1,120	2,030	3,290	6,770	12,300	19,500
1,700	NA	17	32	66	98	189	302	533	1,090	1,970	3,190	6,550	11,900	18,800
1,800	NA	16	31	64	95	184	293	517	1,050	1,910	3,090	6,350	11,500	18,300
1,900	NA	16	30	62	93	178	284	502	1,020	1,850	3,000	6,170	11,200	17,700
2,000	NA	16	29	60	90	173	276	488	1,000	1,800	2,920	6,000	10,900	17,200

For SI: 1 inch = 25.4 mm, 1 foot = 304.8 mm, 1 pound per square inch = 6.895 kPa, 1-inch water column = 0.2488 kPa, 1 British thermal unit per hour = 0.2931 W, 1 cubic foot per hour = 0.0283 m³/h, 1 degree = 0.01745 rad.

Notes:
1. NA means a flow of less than 10 cfh.
2. All table entries have been rounded to three significant digits.

When using corrugated stainless steel tubing (CSST) for gas piping, the manufacturer's tables must be used for sizing purposes.

Topic: Maximum Operating Pressure
Reference: IFGC 402.7
Category: Gas Piping Installations
Subject: Pipe Sizing

Code Text: *The maximum operating pressure for piping systems located inside buildings shall not exceed 5 pounds per square inch gauge (psig) (34 kPa guage) except where one or more of the following conditions are met:*

1. *The piping joints are welded or brazed.*
2. *The piping is joined by fittings listed to ANSI LC-4/CSA 6.32 and installed in accordance with the manufacturer's instructions.*
3. *The piping joints are flanged and pipe-to-flange connections are made by welding or brazing.*
4. *The piping is located in a ventilated chase or otherwise enclosed for protection against accidental gas accumulation.*
5. *The piping is located inside buildings or separate areas of buildings used exclusively for any of the following:*
    5.1. *Industrial processing or heating.*
    5.1. *Research.*
    5.3. *Warehousing.*
    5.4. *Boiler or mechanical rooms.*
6. *The piping is a temporary installation for buildings under construction.*
7. *The piping serves appliances or equipment used for agricultural purposes.*
8. *The piping system is an LP-gas piping system with an operating pressure greater than 20 psi (137.9 kPa) and complies with NFPA 58.*

Discussion and Commentary: Generally, indoor piping systems are limited to a maximum pressure of 5 pounds per square inch gauge. There are a number of exceptions that permit pressure above 5 psig because the prescribed controls reduce the risk of a leak. For example, if a piping system is welded or installed in a separate ventilated chase or enclosure the gas pressure is permitted to exceed 5 psig because a hazardous leak that is due to the increased pressure is not likely to occur. In addition, because of the volume of space and additional safeguards in large industrial, research and warehouse occupancies, which may require systems with higher pressures, these occupancies also are exempt from the maximum 5 psig requirement.

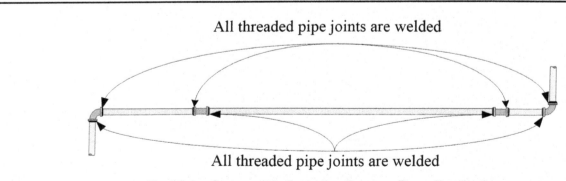

Gas Piping System with Operating Pressure Exceeding 5 psig

LP gas systems are not subject to the 5 psig limit on operating pressures, provided that the design pressure of the system is greater than 20 psig and the system conforms to the installation requirements of NFPA 58.

Topic: General Requirements	**Category:** Gas Piping Installations
Reference: IFGC 403.1	**Subject:** Piping Materials

Code Text: *Materials used for piping systems shall comply with the requirements of this chapter or shall be approved.*

Discussion and Commentary: The code permits certain metallic and nonmetallic piping, tubing, joints and fittings for fuel gas piping. Traditional Schedule 40 steel piping is the most recognizable, as it has been used for many years with proven reliability and durability. Other materials may have thinner walls or be more susceptible to damage when not protected or installed properly, but these materials are designed for safe performance in gas piping systems when installed in accordance with the manufacturer's installation instructions, the provisions of the applicable standards and the requirements of the code. Piping systems that do not entirely conform to the code prescribed materials and methods must be specifically approved by the code official. Cast iron pipe does not perform satisfactorily for gas piping and is expressly prohibited by the code.

Piping materials that do not conform to one of the standards listed by the code require a recommendation by the manufacturer that the material is intended for gas piping, adequate testing to verify that the material will perform safely and approval by the code official.

Study Session 4

Topic: Metallic Pipe Joints
Reference: IFGC 403.9.1
Category: Gas Piping Installations
Subject: Piping Materials

Code Text: *Schedule 40 and heavier pipe joints shall be threaded, flanged, brazed, welded or assembled with press-connect fittings listed in accordance with ANSI LC-4/CSA 6.32. Pipe lighter than Schedule 40 shall be connected using press-connect fittings, flanges, brazing or welding. Where nonferrous pipe is brazed, the brazing materials shall have a melting point in excess of 1,000°F (538°C). Brazing alloys shall not contain more than 0.05- percent phosphorus.*

Discussion and Commentary: Schedule 40 black iron pipe is commonly used for gas piping systems. It typically is joined with threaded fittings or, for larger diameter pipe sizes, has welded joints. Other pipe joint methods are also approved. The code also permits lighter schedule (thinner wall) rigid metallic gas piping such as copper, and schedule 10 steel and stainless steel pipe. Threaded fittings are not allowed for these lighter piping materials.

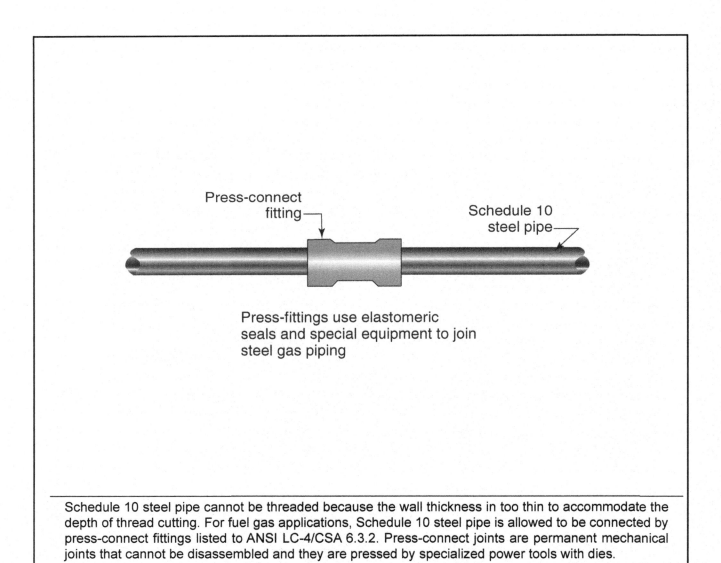

Schedule 10 steel pipe cannot be threaded because the wall thickness in too thin to accommodate the depth of thread cutting. For fuel gas applications, Schedule 10 steel pipe is allowed to be connected by press-connect fittings listed to ANSI LC-4/CSA 6.3.2. Press-connect joints are permanent mechanical joints that cannot be disassembled and they are pressed by specialized power tools with dies.

Topic: Prohibited Locations
Reference: IFGC 404.3
Category: Gas Piping Installations
Subject: Piping System Installation

Code Text: *Piping shall not be installed in or through a ducted supply, return or exhaust, or a clothes chute, chimney or gas vent, dumbwaiter or elevator shaft. Piping installed downstream of the point of delivery shall not extend through any townhouse unit other than the unit served by such piping.*

Discussion and Commentary: Installation of gas piping in or through a circulating duct may cause corrosion to the pipe from condensation that is due to temperature changes and may also affect the performance and maintenance of the ducted air system. A duct or shaft also provides a path for leaking gas to spread throughout the building.

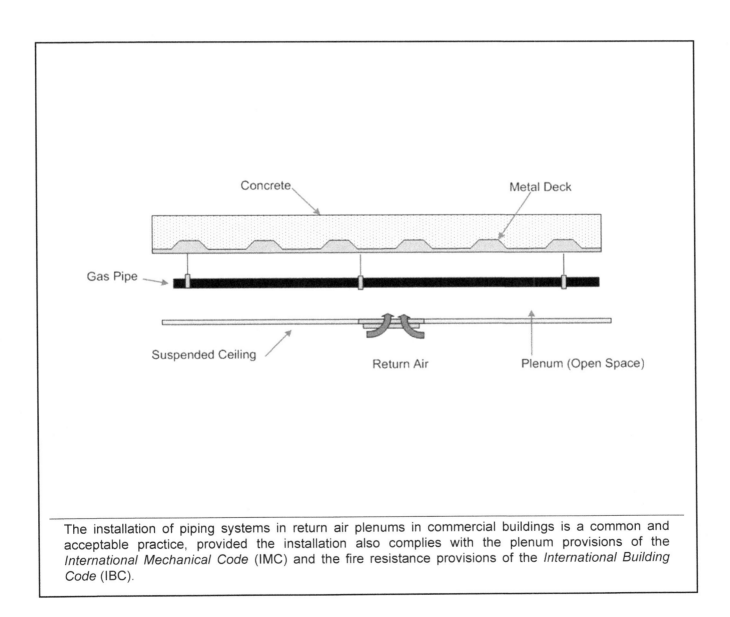

The installation of piping systems in return air plenums in commercial buildings is a common and acceptable practice, provided the installation also complies with the plenum provisions of the *International Mechanical Code* (IMC) and the fire resistance provisions of the *International Building Code* (IBC).

Topic: Fittings in Concealed Locations
Reference: IFGC 404.5
Category: Gas Piping Installations
Subject: Piping System Installation

Code Text: *Fittings installed in concealed locations shall be limited to the following types: (1) Threaded elbows, tees, couplings, plugs and caps; (2) Brazed fittings, (3) Welded fittings, (4) Fittings listed to ANSI LC-1/CSA 6.26 or ANSI LC-4/CSA 6.32.*

Discussion and Commentary: Certain types of fittings require access for inspection and maintenance. For example, unions are not allowed to be installed in concealed locations, because of the potential leaking over time. The most common types of fittings in concealed locations are threaded elbows, tees and couplings for Schedule 40 steel piping. The code also allows brazed and welded fittings. In addition, fittings that are specifically listed for installation in concealed locations, for example Corrugated Stainless Steel Tubing (CSST) gas piping systems, are also permitted.

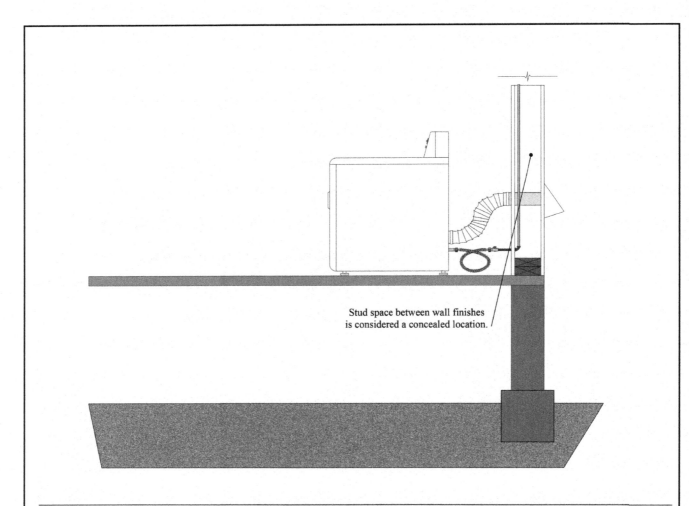

Stud space between wall finishes is considered a concealed location.

A concealed location is one that cannot be accessed without damaging permanent construction, such as a space concealed by finished drywall. Removable ceiling tile or panels are not considered to be creating a concealed space.

Topic: Protection Against Physical Damage **Category:** Gas Piping Installations
Reference: IFGC 404.7 **Subject:** Piping System Installation

Code Text: *Where piping will be concealed within light-frame construction assemblies, the piping shall be protected against penetration by fasteners ... Where piping is installed through holes or notches in framing members and the piping is located less than $1^1/_2$ inches (38 mm) from the framing member face to which wall, ceiling or floor membranes will be attached, the pipe shall be protected by shield plates that cover the width of the pipe and the framing member and that extend not less than 4 inches (51 mm) to each side of the framing member. Where the framing member that the piping passes through is a bottom plate, bottom track, top plate or top track, the shield plates shall cover the framing member and extend not less than 4 inches (51 mm) above the bottom framing member and not less than 4 inches (51 mm) below the top framing member. See the exception for steel piping.*

Discussion and Commentary: Gas piping installed in concealed locations and less than $1^1/_2$ inches from the face of the framing member is subject to nail or screw penetration when the finish material, such as drywall, is installed. The code addresses those locations most susceptible to damage, such as piping passing through holes in wall studs or plates or passing through holes in floor joists or beams. Where the $1^1/_2$-inch clearance is not provided, steel shield plates are required to cover and extend 4 inches beyond the affected area. The protection requirements only apply to concealed gas piping such as aluminum or copper, not steel piping, which sufficiently resists penetration from fasteners. CSST installations must be protected in accordance with the manufacturer's instructions.

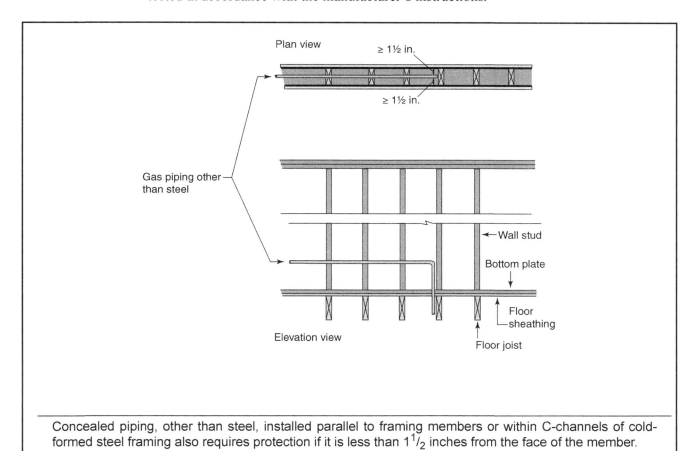

Concealed piping, other than steel, installed parallel to framing members or within C-channels of cold-formed steel framing also requires protection if it is less than $1^1/_2$ inches from the face of the member.

Topic: Piping in Solid Floors
Reference: IFGC 404.8

Category: Gas Piping Installations
Subject: Piping System Installation

Code Text: *Piping in solid floors shall be laid in channels in the floor and covered in a manner that will allow access to the piping with a minimum amount of damage to the building. Where such piping is subject to exposure to excessive moisture or corrosive substances, the piping shall be protected in an approved manner. As an alternative to installation in channels, the piping shall be installed in a conduit of Schedule 40 steel, wrought iron, PVC or ABS pipe in accordance with Section 404.8.1 or 404.8.2.*

Discussion and Commentary: Embedding gas piping in solid concrete floors would subject it to stresses and possible damage from expansion, contraction, shifting or settlement of the concrete floor. Installation of fuel gas piping in a conduit or a channel system protects the pipe from these stresses and prevents damage to the piping system.

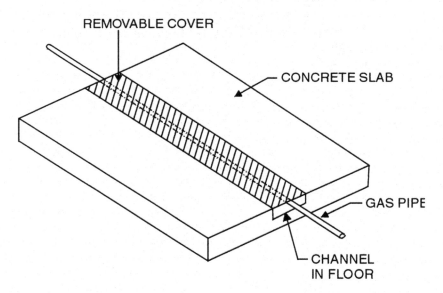

When installing a channel type of system in a solid floor, access is required by means of removable panels.

Topic: Minimum Burial Depth
Reference: IFGC 404.12
Category: Gas Piping Installations
Subject: Piping System Installation

Code Text: *Underground piping systems shall be installed a minimum depth of 12 inches (305 mm) below grade. Individual lines to outside lights, grills or other appliances shall be installed a minimum of 8 inches (203 mm) below finished grade, provided that such installation is approved and is installed in locations not susceptible to physical damage.*

Discussion and Commentary: Fuel gas piping is commonly buried underground in outdoor locations for convenience, aesthetics, protection from damage and to prevent tampering. The 12-inch minimum burial depth allows typical yard work and gardening without the worker coming into contact with buried gas piping.

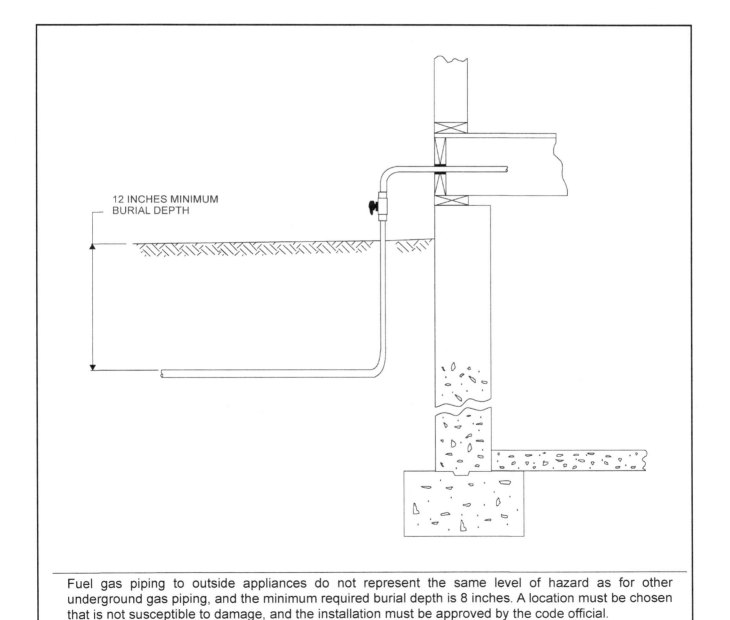

Fuel gas piping to outside appliances do not represent the same level of hazard as for other underground gas piping, and the minimum required burial depth is 8 inches. A location must be chosen that is not susceptible to damage, and the installation must be approved by the code official.

Topic: General
Reference: IFGC 406.1

Category: Gas Piping Installations
Subject: Inspection, Testing and Purging

Code Text: *Prior to acceptance and initial operation, all piping installations shall be inspected and pressure tested to determine that the materials, design, fabrication and installation practices comply with the requirements of this code.*

Discussion and Commentary: Pressure testing of the gas piping system ensures its safe operation without leaks when put into service. Air and inert gases are the only acceptable test mediums. The code prescribes the method of measurement, the minimum test pressure and the test duration. Purging is necessary before the gas piping system is placed in operation and involves displacing the air in the piping with natural gas at a continuous flow. Larger piping systems or those under greater pressure require purging with an inert gas before natural gas is introduced into the system.

Oxygen significantly accelerates the burning of any fuel and is strictly prohibited from being used for pressure testing or purging of gas piping systems.

Topic: Leak Detection Methods
Reference: IFGC 406.5.1
Category: Gas Piping Installations
Subject: Inspection, Testing and Purging

Code Text: *The leakage shall be located by means of an approved gas detector, a noncorrosive leak detection fluid or other approved leak detection methods.*

Discussion and Commentary: If the gas piping being tested fails to maintain the test pressure, the leaks must be located and repaired, and the piping retested. Typically, while compressed air is in the piping system, an approved noncorrosive liquid soap solution is applied to the joints or any suspected areas of leakage. Bubbles indicate the location of the leak. Once leaks are repaired, the piping system must be pressure tested again to verify there are no drops in pressure before placing the piping into service.

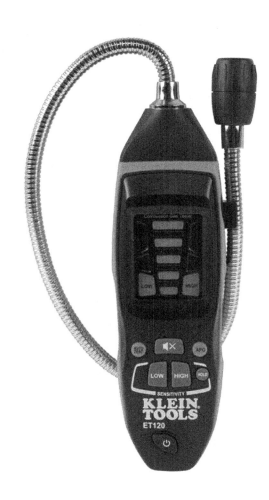

An approved electronic gas detector and noncorrosive liquid soap solutions are the approved methods for safely detecting leaking fuel gas. There have been many accidents and injuries caused by using open flame to detect leaks in fuel gas systems. *(Photo courtesy of Klein Tools.)*

Study Session 4
IFGC Sections 401 through 406

1. For other than steel piping and CSST, exposed gas piping must be identified by a yellow label marked "Gas" in black letters and the markings spaced at intervals not exceeding _____ feet.

    a. 5
    b. 10
    c. 15
    d. 20

    Reference _____

2. Where there are multiple meters, the _____ must mark the piping system supplied by each meter with an approved permanent identification.

    a. owner
    b. gas supplier
    c. installer
    d. code official

    Reference _____

3. The volume of gas to be provided must be determined directly from the _____ of the appliance served.

    a. input rating
    b. output rating
    c. hourly load
    d. operating pressure

    Reference _____

4. Gas piping is permitted to be sized in accordance with the sizing tables of the _____.

   a. gas supplier
   b. piping system manufacturer
   c. approved testing agency
   d. piping supplier

   Reference _____

5. Using the longest length method for sizing gas piping, each section of piping is measured from _____.

   a. the first branch to the appliance
   b. the point of delivery to the most remote outlet
   c. the point of delivery to the first branch
   d. the pressure regulator to the most remote outlet

   Reference _____

6. A gas piping system located inside a(n) _____ building is limited to a maximum design operating pressure of 5 pounds per square inch gage (psig).

   a. institutional   b. industrial
   c. warehouse   d. research

   Reference _____

7. Used pipe, fittings, valves and other materials must not be used in a gas piping system except where they are free of _____.

   a. paint   b. corrosion
   c. foreign material d. abrasion

   Reference _____

8. Copper and copper alloy gas piping is permitted to be installed when the gas contains no more than an average of _____ grains of hydrogen sulfide per 100 standard cubic feet of gas.

   a. 0.9   b. 0.6
   c. 0.3   d. 0.1

   Reference _____

9. Field drilled and tapped pipe fittings are permitted under limited conditions when the work is performed by _____.

   a. a licensed pipefitter

   b. the contractor holding the permit

   c. an approved third-party agency

   d. the gas supplier

   Reference _____

10. For steel gas piping, threaded fittings larger than _____ inches are not permitted.

    a. 2
    b. 2½
    c. 3
    d. 4

    Reference _____

11. Gas piping must not be installed in or through a(n) _____.

    a. plenum
    b. clothes chute
    c. attic
    d. enclosed space

    Reference _____

12. _____ piping is not allowed for supplying fuel gas.

    a. Aluminum
    b. Copper alloy
    c. CPVC
    d. Polyethylene

    Reference _____

13. Portions of gas piping systems installed in concealed locations must not have _____.

    a. unions
    b. threaded fittings
    c. welded joints
    d. brazed fittings

    Reference _____

14. Gas piping must not enter a building _____.

    a. underground
    b. through a foundation
    c. above grade
    d. without a sleeve

    Reference _____

15. Where gas piping is required to be installed in conduit and one end terminates outdoors, the conduit must extend not less than _____ inches outside the building.

    a. 2   b. 4
    c. 8   d. 12

    Reference _____

16. A required conduit containing gas piping must extend not less than _____ inches beyond the point where the pipe emerges from the floor in the building.

    a. 10   b. 6
    c. 2   d. 3

    Reference _____

17. Exterior above-ground gas piping must be elevated not less than _____ inches above ground and roof surfaces.

    a. $3^{1}/_{2}$ b. 3
    c. $2^{1}/_{2}$ d. 2

    Reference _____

18. In general, underground gas piping systems must be installed at a minimum depth of _____ inches below grade.

    a. 12   b. 15
    c. 18   d. 24

    Reference _____

19. The unthreaded portion of gas piping outlets must extend not less than _____ inch(es) through finished ceilings and walls.

    a. 4   b. 3
    c. 2   d. 1

    Reference _____

20. Plastic gas pipe is generally permitted to be installed_____.

    a. outdoors underground only

    b. outdoors underground or above ground

    c. where protected from physical damage

    d. indoors when installed in a conduit

    Reference_____

21. Underground nonmetallic gas piping requires a yellow insulated copper tracer wire not less than size_____.

    a. 12 AWG   b. 14 AWG

    c. 18 AWG   d. 20 AWG

    Reference_____

22. The following threaded fittings for steel gas piping are allowed in concealed locations except _____.

    a. couplings   b. tees

    c. unions   d. elbows

    Reference_____

23. The test duration for testing a gas piping system with a volume less than 10 cubic feet must be not less than _____ minutes.

    a. 60   b. 30

    c. 10   d. 5

    Reference_____

24. The test pressure must be not less than _____ times the proposed maximum working pressure of the gas piping system.

    a. 3   b. $2\frac{1}{2}$

    c. 2   d. $1\frac{1}{2}$

    Reference_____

25. Where steel shield plates are required to protect concealed gas piping installed through holes in wood studs, the shield plates must extend a minimum of _____ inches to each side of the stud.

　　a. 4　　　　　　　　　　　　b. 6

　　c. 1½　　　　　　　　　　　d. 2

　　Reference_____

Study Session 5

2021 IFGC Sections 407 through 416
Gas Piping Installations II

OBJECTIVE: To gain an understanding of the installation requirements for fuel gas piping systems, including provisions for piping supports, shutoff valves, regulators and connections to appliances.

REFERENCE: Sections 407 through 416, 2021 *International Fuel Gas Code*

KEY POINTS:
- What are the requirements for supporting gas piping?
- Where are drips required in gas piping systems?
- Where are sediment traps required in gas piping systems?
- What standards are mandated for gas shutoff valves?
- On what side of a meter should a shutoff be located?
- Where are shutoff valves required?
- What are the location requirements for shutoff valves in relation to an appliance?
- When may a gas shutoff be located in an area remote from the appliance?
- Are pressure regulators required to be listed?
- What are the termination requirements for a vent on a pressure regulator?
- Vent piping for relief vents and breather vents shall be constructed of what materials?
- What type of connector is required for appliances equipped with casters or subject to periodic moving?
- When is physical protection required for gas connectors and tubing?
- What is the maximum length permitted for a gas connector?
- How are gas connectors required to be sized?
- Where are shutoff valves required to be located in relation to a gas appliance connector?
- What location and safety requirements apply to LP-gas motor vehicle fuel-dispensing facilities?

KEY POINTS:
(Cont'd)
- What are the requirements for emergency shutdown devices for a compressed natural gas motor vehicle fuel dispenser?
- A vent tube for a compressed natural gas motor vehicle fuel dispensing facility is regulated by what code?
- When are approved "NO SMOKING" signs required?

Topic: Design and Installation	**Category:** Gas Piping Installations
Reference: IFGC 407.2	**Subject:** Piping Support

Code Text: *Piping shall be supported with metal pipe hooks, metal pipe straps, metal bands, metal brackets, metal hangers or building structural components, suitable for the size of piping, of adequate strength and quality, and located at intervals so as to prevent or damp out excessive vibration. Piping shall be anchored to prevent undue strains on connected appliances and shall not be supported by other piping. Pipe hangers and supports shall conform to the requirements of MSS SP-58 and shall be spaced in accordance with Section 415. Supports, hangers and anchors shall be installed so as not to interfere with the free expansion and contraction of the piping between anchors. All parts of the supporting equipment shall be designed and installed so they will not be disengaged by movement of the supported piping.*

Discussion and Commentary: Piping supports are designed to carry the weight of the piping and its content, and to align and slope the pipe to prevent accumulation of moisture. Proper support prevents excessive movement of the piping and undue strain on the appliance connections. Properly designed pipe supports accommodate for the expansion and contraction of the materials used in constructing the fuel gas piping system. Piping must have its own dedicated support system and not be supported by electrical conduits, duct work or other building utility systems.

Pipe supports must be of a material that will be compatible with the pipe being supported. If the piping system and hanger system are in contact with each other and have dissimilar metals, corrosion may result and cause the pipe to fail.

Topic: Sediment Traps
Reference: IFGC 408.4

Category: Gas Piping Installations
Subject: Drips and Sloped Piping

Code Text: *Where a sediment trap is not incorporated as part of the appliance, a sediment trap shall be installed downstream of the appliance shutoff valve as close to the inlet of the appliance as practical. The sediment trap shall be either a tee fitting having a capped nipple of any length installed vertically in the bottommost opening of the tee as illustrated in Figure 408.4 or other device approved as an effective sediment trap. Illuminating appliances, ranges, clothes dryers, decorative vented appliances for installation in vented fireplaces, gas fireplaces, and outdoor grills need not be so equipped.*

Discussion and Commentary: Sediment traps are a vertical length of capped pipe located below the lowest section of pipe and installed adjacent to most appliances to trap any debris in the piping before it reaches the appliance and causes damage. Over its service life, moisture resulting from condensation or the introduction of air into the system when connections are made or broken may accumulate in sediment traps.

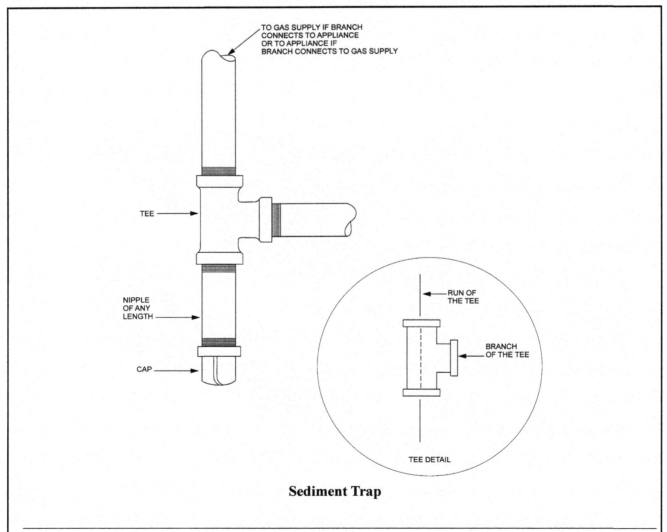

Sediment Trap

Debris in the gas lines can cause an appliance to malfunction, operate inefficiently or create hazardous conditions if unwanted particles find their way into the controls or burners of the appliance.

Topic: Valve Approval
Reference: IFGC 409.1.1
Category: Gas Piping Installations
Subject: Shutoff Valves

Code Text: *Shutoff valves shall be of an approved type; shall be constructed of materials compatible with the piping; and shall comply with the standard that is applicable for the pressure and application, in accordance with Table 409.1.1.*

Discussion and Commentary: Shutoff valves must be approved for the particular application and meet the requirements of Table 409.1.1, Manual Gas Valve Standards. The table identifies the appropriate standard for the application and maximum gas pressure.

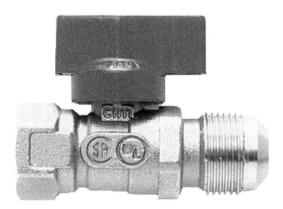

Most shutoff valves are of the ball type because of their proven reliability.

Topic: Multiple-tenant Buildings
Reference: IFGC 409.3.1
Category: Gas Piping Installations
Subject: Shutoff Valves

Code Text: *In multiple-tenant buildings, where a common piping system is installed to supply other than one- and two-family dwellings, shutoff valves shall be provided for each tenant. Each tenant shall have access to the shutoff valve serving that tenant's space.*

Discussion and Commentary: A shutoff valve is required for each tenant or dwelling unit in a building. This allows the individual system to be isolated from the common system with the gas supply to the space controlled by the tenant. Service and repairs may be performed on the piping system serving each dwelling or sleeping unit without turning off the gas supply serving the entire building.

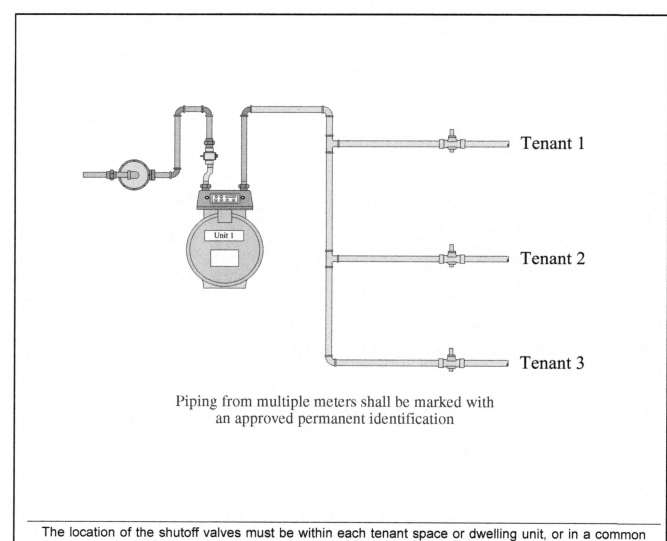

Piping from multiple meters shall be marked with an approved permanent identification

The location of the shutoff valves must be within each tenant space or dwelling unit, or in a common area that is accessible to all the tenants.

Topic: Appliance Shutoff Valve Location
Category: Gas Piping Installations
Reference: IFGC 409.5.1
Subject: Shutoff Valves

Code Text: *The shutoff valve shall be located in the same room as the appliance. The shutoff valve shall be within 6 feet (1829 mm) of the appliance, and shall be installed upstream of the union, connector or quick disconnect device it serves. Such shutoff valves shall be provided with access. Shutoff valves serving movable appliances, such as cooking appliances and clothes dryers, shall be considered to be provided with access where installed behind such appliances. Appliance shutoff valves located in the firebox of a fireplace shall be installed in accordance with the appliance manufacturer's instructions.*

Discussion and Commentary: A shutoff valve shall not serve more than one appliance and must be located where it is accessible to tenants or maintenance personnel. In the case of an appliance installation, the shutoff valve must be located in the same room and within 6 feet of the appliance. Providing the shutoff upstream of the connector or union permits the gas supply to the appliance to be turned off for service, repair or replacement of the appliance and the connector. Without this provision, the entire gas supply to the building would require shutdown for work on one appliance.

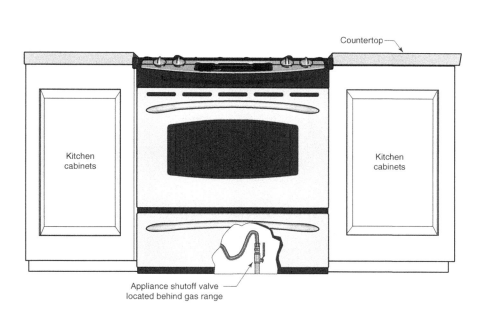

Shutoff valves behind movable appliances are considered as meeting the requirement for access.

Access is required to all shutoff valves for ease of locating and operating the valve for maintenance, replacement or repair to the fuel gas system downstream of the valve, or as needed to turn off the gas supply in an emergency situation. Shutoff valves behind movable appliances are considered as complying with the access requirements.

Topic: Tubing Systems
Reference: IFGC 409.7
Category: Gas Piping Installations
Subject: Shutoff Valves

Code Text: *Shutoff valves installed in tubing systems shall be rigidly and securely supported independently of the tubing.*

Discussion and Commentary: Shutoff valves in gas tubing systems require rigid support separate from the tubing to prevent damage at the valve connection. Where tubing is used and the shutoff valve connects to rigid piping on the outlet side of the valve, the rigid piping provides secure support that is not susceptible to damage. However, if a shutoff valve is installed in a run of CSST or other tubing material, the torque applied to the valve rotating member will transfer to the tubing causing stress and possible failure. The code requirement is consistent with manufacturers' installation instructions for CSST.

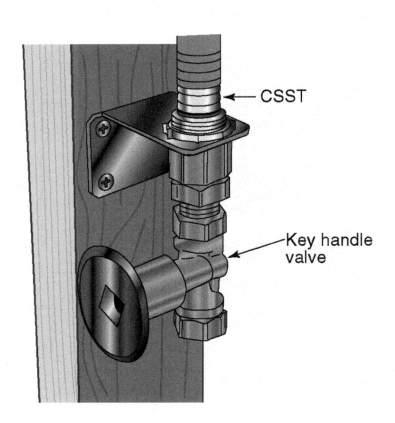

A shutoff valve, such as a concealed T-handle keyed valve for a fireplace, installed in a run of CSST or other tubing material must be supported independently of the tubing to prevent damage to the tubing.

Topic: Pressure Regulators
Reference: IFGC 410.1
Category: Gas Piping Installations
Subject: Flow Controls

Code Text: *A line pressure regulator shall be installed where the appliance is designed to operate at a lower pressure than the supply pressure. Line gas pressure regulators shall be listed as complying with ANSI Z21.80/CSA 6.22. Access shall be provided to pressure regulators. Pressure regulators shall be protected from physical damage. Regulators installed on the exterior of the building shall be approved for outdoor installation.*

Discussion and Commentary: Regulators reduce the service delivery pressure to the pressure of the distribution system. The distribution system pressure can then be reduced even further by the regulators in the appliance or other regulators installed at points along the system.

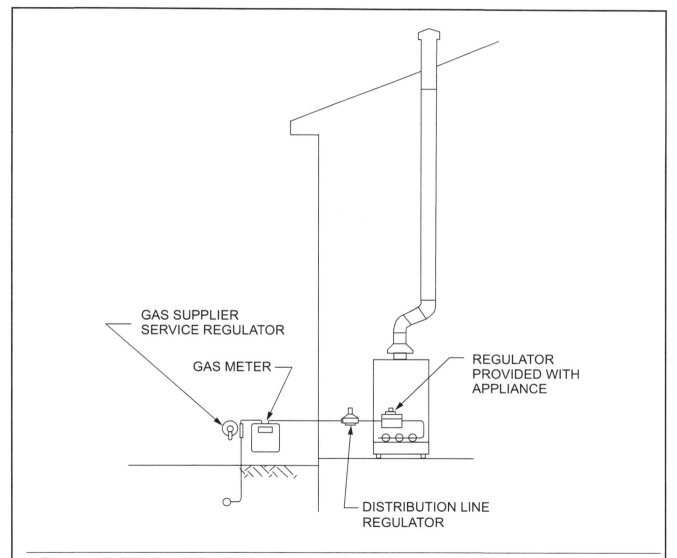

Pressure regulators are devices that help protect appliances from damage and improper operation that are due to pressures exceeding the design limit of the appliance. Excessive pressures may create a hazardous condition.

Topic: Venting of Regulators
Reference: IFGC 410.3

Category: Gas Piping Installations
Subject: Flow Controls

Code Text: *Pressure regulators that require a vent shall be vented directly to the outdoors. The vent shall be designed to prevent the entry of insects, water and foreign objects.* See the exception for using an approved vent-limiting device installed in accordance with the manufacturer's instructions.

Discussion and Commentary: A pressure regulator is a valve that automatically cuts off the flow of a liquid or gas at a certain pressure. Regulators are used to allow high-pressure fluid supply lines or tanks to be reduced to safe and/or usable pressures for various applications.

All fuel gas applications require the use of a regulator. Because pressures in LP-gas containers can fluctuate significantly, regulators must be present to deliver a steady flow pressure to downstream appliances. These regulators normally compensate for pressures from as little as 30 psig to in excess of 200 psig and commonly deliver 11 inches of water column for residential applications and 35 inches of water column (27.7 inches of water column equals 1 pound per square inch) for industrial applications. Pressure regulators differ in size and shape, delivery pressure and adjustability but are uniform in their purpose to deliver a constant outlet pressure for downstream requirements. For all regulators the outlet pressure is lower than inlet pressure.

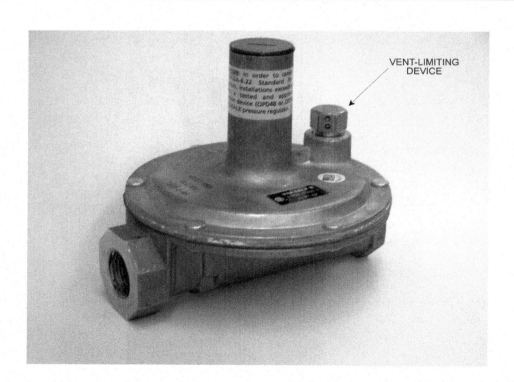

An exception to venting to the outdoors permits a pressure regulator with a vent-limiting device. Care must be taken to install these units following the manufacturer's installation instructions.

Topic: Connecting Appliances
Reference: IFGC 411.1
Category: Gas Piping Installations
Subject: Appliance Connections

Code Text: *Except as required by Section 411.1.1, appliances shall be connected to the piping system by one of the following:* The list includes (1) Rigid metallic pipe and fittings, (2) Corrugated stainless steel tubing (CSST), (3) Semirigid metallic tubing and metallic fittings, (4) Listed and labeled appliance connectors in compliance with ANSI Z21.24, (5) Listed and labeled quick-disconnect devices in compliance with ANSI Z21.41/CGA 6.9 used in conjunction with listed and labeled appliance connectors, (6) Listed and labeled convenience outlets in compliance with ANSI Z21.90/CGA 6.24 used in conjunction with listed and labeled appliance connectors, (7) Listed and labeled outdoor appliance connectors in compliance with ANSI Z21.75/CSA 6.27, (8) Listed outdoor gas hose connectors in compliance with ANZI Z21.54 used to connect portable outdoor appliances, and (9) Gas hose connectors for use in laboratories and education facilities.

Discussion and Commentary: Connectors are used to connect the appliance or equipment to the gas distribution system. Connector types vary with the particular application, from commercial cooking equipment that is moved away from the wall for cleaning to a fixed residential type horizontal furnace in an attic. The type of appliance must be taken into consideration when selecting a connector that attaches to the gas distribution system.

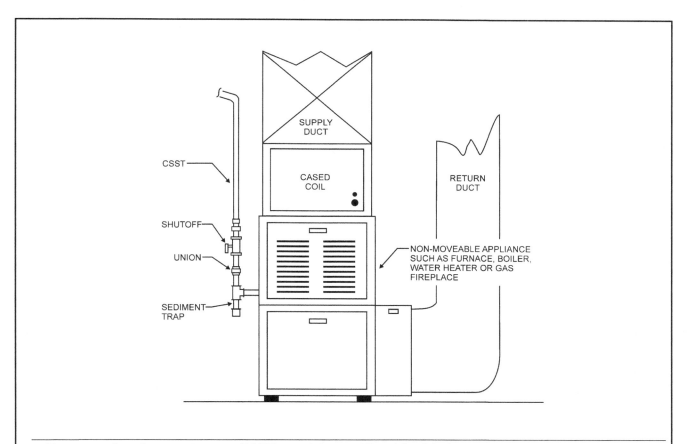

Two examples of connectors are CSST gas piping and listed flexible fuel gas connectors. The appliance also may be connected to the gas piping with rigid metallic pipe as shown in the illustration.

Topic: Prohibited Locations and Penetrations   **Category:** Gas Piping Installations
Reference: IFGC 411.1.3.3   **Subject:** Appliance Connections

Code Text: *Connectors shall not be concealed within, or extended through, walls, floors, partitions, ceilings or appliance housings.* See the exceptions for 1) Connectors constructed of materials allowed for piping systems shall be permitted to pass through walls, floors, partitions and ceilings for vented decorative appliances and manifolds. 2) Rigid steel pipe connectors shall be permitted to extend through openings in appliance housings. 3) Fireplace inserts that are factory equipped with grommets, sleeves or other means of protection in accordance with the listing of the appliance. 4) Semirigid tubing and listed connectors shall be permitted to extend through an opening in an appliance housing, cabinet or casing where the tubing or connector is protected against damage.

Discussion and Commentary: In most cases, the appliance shutoff valve and the appliance connector downstream of the shutoff valve must be in the same room as the appliance, and the code prohibits the connector from passing through walls, floors or ceilings. In addition, connectors are not permitted to extend through appliance housings, because of potential damage from contact with sharp edges or abrasion through movement or vibration. Exception 2 recognizes that rigid steel piping used as a connector is not susceptible to such damage. Exception 4 allows semirigid tubing and listed connectors to extend through appliance housings when protected against damage, typically with a sleeve or grommet. In the case of fireplace inserts as provided in Exception 3, any type of approved gas piping may extend through the housing if the sleeve or grommet is factory installed.

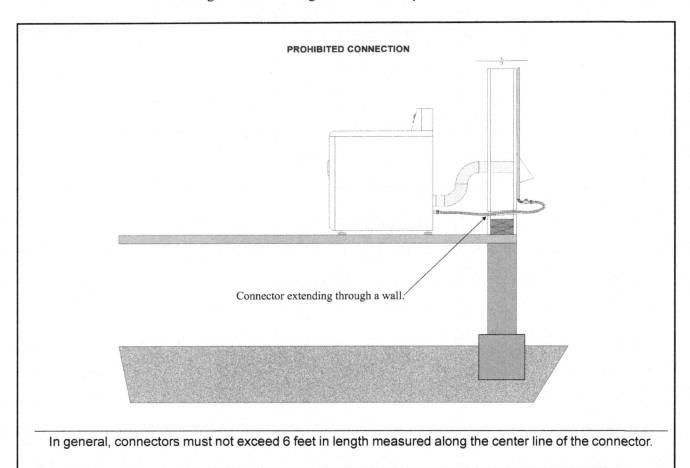

In general, connectors must not exceed 6 feet in length measured along the center line of the connector.

Topic: Movable Appliances
Reference: IFGC 411.1.4
Category: Gas Piping Installations
Subject: Appliance Connections

Code Text: *Where appliances are equipped with casters or are otherwise subject to periodic movement or relocation for purposes such as routine cleaning and maintenance, such appliances shall be connected to the supply system piping by means of an appliance connector listed as complying with ANZI Z21.69/CSA 6.16 or by means of Item 1 of Section 411.1. Such flexible connectors shall be installed and protected against physical damage in accordance with the manufacturer's instructions.*

Discussion and Commentary: Equipment subject to moving for the purposes of maintenance or cleaning requires a gas connector designed for that type of application. Over time, the frequent movement of an appliance may cause the failure of a connector. These special purpose connectors require a label that identifies the application for appliances that are routinely moved.

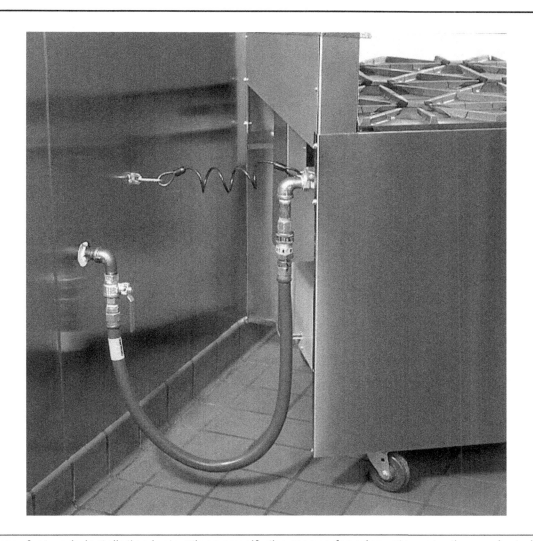

The manufacturer's installation instructions specify the means for adequate protection against physical damage to connectors for movable equipment.

Study Session 5

Topic: Attendants
Reference: IFGC 412.5
Category: Gas Piping Installations
Subject: LPG Motor Vehicle Fuel-Dispensing Facilities

Code Text: *Motor vehicle fueling operations shall be conducted by qualified attendants or in accordance with Section 412.9 by persons trained in the proper handling of LP-gas.*

Discussion and Commentary: LP-gas dispensing station operations are regulated by the IFGC and the *International Fire Code* (IFC), both of which set forth restrictions for public access and other fire and life safety provisions. One of those provisions requires LP gas for motor vehicles to be dispensed by persons who are trained in the proper handling of LP gas.

Section 412.9 does permit self-service LP-gas dispensing systems for use by trained individuals in fueling private vehicles, provided certain safeguards are in place such as restricted access requiring a code, key or card to operate the equipment, and installation of an emergency shutoff switch. In addition the system must be designed and maintained for safe operation. The owner of the facility is responsible for ensuring proper training of users.

Topic: Separation
Category: Gas Piping Installations
Reference: IFGC 413.10.2.3
Subject: CNG Motor Vehicle Fuel-Dispensing Facilities

Code Text: *The structure or appurtenance used for stabilizing the cylinder shall be separated from the site equipment, features and exposures and shall be located in accordance with Table 413.10.2.3.*

Discussion and Commentary: Compressed Natural Gas (CNG) motor vehicle fuel dispensing facilities are regulated by the IFGC and the *International Fire Code* (IFC). The IFGC restricts the location of CNG compression, storage and dispensing equipment and contains provisions for residential fueling appliance installation. Self-service fueling facilities require similar safeguards to those in place for LP-gas vehicle dispensing facilities. Section 413.10.2.3 applies to the atmospheric venting of motor vehicle fuel cylinders and requires that the location of the cylinders (vessels) being vented must be separated a minimum distance from buildings, building openings, lot lines, public ways, vehicles and other CNG equipment.

[F] TABLE 413.10.2.3
SEPARATION DISTANCE FOR
ATMOSPHERIC VENTING OF CNG

EQUIPMENT OR FEATURE	MINIMUM SEPARATION (feet)
Buildings	25
Building openings	25
Lot lines	15
Public ways	15
Vehicles	25
CNG compressor and storage vessels	25
CNG dispensers	25

For SI: 1 foot = 304.8 mm.

Because of the volatility of highly pressurized CNG in cylinders, atmospheric venting of the containers requires a separation distance of 15 feet from lot lines and public ways, and 25 feet from buildings, vehicles, compressors, storage vessels and CNG dispensers.

Quiz

Study Session 5
IFGC Sections 407 through 416

1. Supports for 1-inch steel gas piping shall be spaced no more than _____ feet apart.

    a. 4   b. 6

    c. 8   d. 10

    Reference _____

2. Gas piping supports for $1/2$-inch copper tubing shall be spaced no more than _____ feet apart.

    a. 4   b. 6

    c. 8   d. 10

    Reference _____

3. Unless incorporated as part of the appliance, a sediment trap shall be installed _____.

    a. downstream of the appliance shutoff valve

    b. remote from the appliance location

    c. upstream of the appliance shutoff valve

    d. upstream of the manifold

    Reference _____

4. Sediment traps are not required for _____.

    a. ranges   b. water heaters

    c. boilers   d. forced air furnaces

    Reference _____

5. The installation of shutoff valves shall be prohibited _____.
   a. in concealed locations
   b. in bedrooms and bathrooms
   c. in furnace room enclosures
   d. on the roof of buildings

   Reference _____

6. Where a single meter is used to supply gas to more than one building, a shutoff valve shall be provided _____.
   a. at the manifold
   b. outdoors at each building
   c. inside at the point of entry to each building
   d. at an approved location

   Reference _____

7. A gas shutoff valve shall be located within _____ feet of the appliance.
   a. 2
   b. 5
   c. 6
   d. 7

   Reference _____

8. When installing a gas shutoff valve for an appliance, the shutoff valve shall be located _____.
   a. upstream of a union
   b. downstream of an appliance connector
   c. downstream of a quick disconnect device
   d. with ready access without removing a panel

   Reference _____

9. A listed outdoor gas hose used to connect a portable outdoor appliance to the gas piping system must comply with _____.
   a. ANSI Z21.69
   b. ANSI Z21.24
   c. ANSI Z21.75
   d. ANSI Z21.54

   Reference _____

10. A shutoff valve for a _____ is permitted to be located in an area remote from the appliance.

    a. range
    b. vented decorative appliance
    c. clothes dryer
    d. water heater

    Reference _____

11. The vent pipe for pressure regulators shall be designed to prevent _____.

    a. the release of fuel gas
    b. back pressure
    c. rupture of the regulator diaphragm
    d. the entry of insects

    Reference _____

12. The appliance shutoff valve is permitted to be installed at a manifold that is not greater than _____ feet from the appliance.

    a. 6
    b. 12
    c. 25
    d. 50

    Reference _____

13. Semirigid metallic tubing used to connect a gas appliance shall not exceed _____ feet in length.

    a. 6
    b. 3
    c. 5
    d. 2

    Reference _____

14. Appliance shutoff valves located at a manifold are not required to be _____.

    a. readily accessible
    b. in the same room as the appliance
    c. identified
    d. protected from damage

    Reference _____

15. A dedicated gas shutoff valve must be located adjacent to the egress door of a laboratory having _____ or more fuel gas outlets.

    a. 4
    b. 2
    c. 8
    d. 6

    Reference _____

16. A vent to the outdoors is not required for a pressure regulator equipped with a _____.

    a. breather vent
    b. vent-limiting device
    c. relief vent
    d. vent manifold

    Reference _____

17. A union must be installed not more than _____ inches from an MP regulator that is connected to rigid piping.

    a. 8
    b. 12
    c. 18
    d. 36

    Reference _____

18. Fuel gas piping for other than dry gas conditions shall be sloped not less than _____ inch in 15 feet to prevent traps.

    a. 1
    b. $3/4$
    c. $1/2$
    d. $1/4$

    Reference _____

19. When a union is provided for an appliance connected by rigid metallic pipe, the union shall be accessible and located within _____ feet of the appliance.

    a. 2
    b. 3
    c. 4
    d. 6

    Reference _____

20. LP-gas motor vehicle fuel-dispensing facilities that are self-service require an emergency shutoff switch located a maximum of _____ feet from the dispenser.

    a. 25   b. 50

    c. 75   d. 100

Reference_____

21. In LP-gas motor vehicle fuel-dispensing facilities, the hose length shall not exceed _____ feet.

    a. 8   b. 12

    c. 18   d. 25

Reference_____

22. Unless located in a vault, CNG storage and dispensing equipment is not permitted to be installed less than _____.

    a. 10 feet from an ignition source

    b. 15 feet from a building

    c. 25 feet from a property line

    d. 50 feet from a public street

Reference_____

23. For appliances designed to operate at 14 inches w.c. or less, overpressure protection devices are required only if the service supply pressure exceeds _____ psi.

    a. 1   b. 2

    c. 4   d. 6

Reference_____

24. Where a residential compressed natural gas (CNG) fueling appliance is located indoors, a methane gas detector shall be located no lower than _____ inches from the highest point of the room or space.

    a. 6   b. 4

    c. 16   d. 12

Reference_____

25. The maximum distance that is allowed between hangers supporting horizontal $1^1/_4$-inch nominal diameter rigid steel pipe used to supply natural gas to an appliance is _____ feet.

    a. 4   b. 6

    c. 10   d. 8

Reference_____

Study Session

6

2021 IFGC Sections 501 through 503.6.14
Chimneys and Vents I

OBJECTIVE: To gain an understanding of the code provisions that minimize the hazards associated with the venting of combustion products, including the proper selection, design, construction, and installation of chimneys and vents.

REFERENCE: Sections 501 through 503.6.14, 2021 *International Fuel Gas Code*

KEY POINTS:
- What requirements apply to masonry chimney construction?
- Venting of appliances using fuels other than fuel gas shall be governed by what code?
- Under what conditions is it permissible to connect an appliance to a flue serving a factory-built fireplace?
- What appliances are not required to be connected to a venting system?
- Are screws, rivets or other fasteners allowed in the connections of a Type B vent?
- What are the limitations for flue lining systems for use with Category I appliances?
- What requirements apply to the design, sizing and installation of vents serving Category II, III or IV appliances?
- What are the listing requirements for Type B and BW vents?
- What are the requirements for protecting vents against physical damage in concealed locations?
- What are the termination requirements for vents serving direct vent appliances?
- What requirements apply to mechanical draft systems, and how do they differ from other venting systems?
- What restrictions apply to a venting system passing through an above-ceiling air plenum?
- What are the various types of venting systems listed in Table 503.4? Which type of venting system applies to each of the appliances listed?
- Under what conditions is plastic pipe allowed to be used to vent a gas appliance?

KEY POINTS:
(Cont'd)

- What provisions apply to the installation of a metal chimney?
- What are the termination requirements for chimneys?
- What provisions apply to an existing chimney when replacing an appliance?
- What items need to be considered when supporting a vent connector?
- What are the spacing requirements for supports of a factory-built chimney?
- What are the requirements for the termination of a gas vent above the roof of a building?
- What are the limitations for the installation of a decorative shroud at the termination of a gas vent?
- What minimum distances apply to the termination of a gas vent in relation to the appliance being vented?
- What is the minimum distance between the termination of a gas vent and any forced air inlet?
- What governs the size of a vent serving an appliance with a natural draft venting system?
- What sizing method applies to a mechanical draft venting system?
- What requirements apply to the installation of a common vent in a multistory building?

Topic: Positive Pressure
Reference: IFGC 501.6
Category: Chimneys and Vents
Subject: General Requirements

Code Text: *Where an appliance equipped with a mechanical forced draft system creates a positive pressure in the venting system, the venting system shall be designed for positive pressure applications.*

Discussion and Commentary: A Type B vent or a similar venting system is not approved for venting appliances with positive pressure venting, because of the increased risk of combustion products being forced back into the building. The venting system must either be listed for positive pressure systems or designed and installed for the specific application in accordance with the recommendations of the appliance manufacturer.

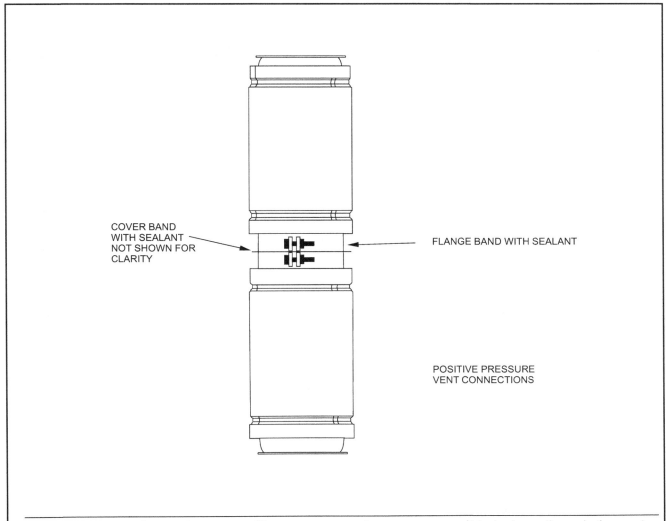

An improper venting system on positive pressure appliances may result in leakage through the vent systems joints. In addition to the risk of introducing harmful products of combustion into the building, leakage at the joints may also produce condensation and cause corrosion of the vent material.

Topic: Appliances Not Required to Be Vented **Category:** Chimneys and Vents
Reference: IFGC 501.8 **Subject:** General Requirements

Code Text: *The following appliances shall not be required to be vented.* The list includes: (1) ranges, (2) built-in domestic cooking units listed and marked for optional venting, (3) hot plates and laundry stoves, (4) Type 1 clothes dryers, (5) a single booster-type automatic instantaneous water heater with specific limitations, (6) refrigerators, (7) counter appliances, (8) room heaters listed for unvented use, (9) direct-fired makeup air heaters, (10) other appliances listed for unvented use and not provided with flue collars, (11) specialized appliances of limited input such as laboratory burners and gas lights.

Discussion and Commentary: Certain appliances with limited input ratings or specialized applications are designed to operate safely without requiring venting systems. The first four appliances in the list (ranges, built-in domestic cooking units, hot plates and laundry stoves, and Type 1 clothes dryers) are exempt from venting requirements when installed in accordance with other provisions of the IFGC. The appliances in the remainder of the list, Items 5 through 11, do not require venting systems, provided the room containing the appliances provides the necessary volume of combustion air. This is similar to the provisions of Section 304.5.1, which is the Standard Method for combustion air, but in this case only the volume of air in the room containing the appliances may be considered, not air from adjoining rooms (adjoining rooms may be included only if connected by a doorway that cannot be closed). If the aggregate input of appliances in the room exceeds the 20 Btu/h per cubic foot volume of the room, then an approved venting system must be installed.

Residential range not required to be vented

Residential ranges are not required to be vented unless specifically required by the manufacturer's installation instructions.

Topic: Connections Exhauster	**Category:** Chimneys and Vents
Reference: IFGC 501.10	**Subject:** General Requirements

Code Text: *Appliance connections to a chimney or vent equipped with a power exhauster shall be made on the inlet side of the exhauster. Joints on the positive pressure side of the exhauster shall be sealed to prevent flue-gas leakage as specified by the manufacturer's installation instructions for the exhauster.*

Discussion and Commentary: When a power exhauster is installed in a vent system, it creates a positive pressure on the outlet side of the fan. To prevent a hazardous condition where products of combustion would be introduced into the building, the appliance connection to the vent must be on the inlet side of the power exhauster device. The venting system on the outlet side of the power exhauster must be listed or approved for such use. Type B venting systems are not approved for this use, because the joints cannot effectively be sealed to prevent the migration of combustion products back into the building under the positive pressure.

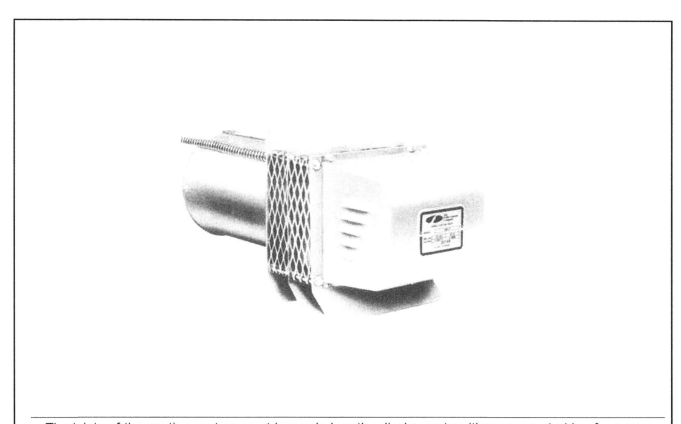

The joints of the venting system must be sealed on the discharge (positive pressure) side of a power exhauster to prevent leakage of flue gases back into the building, thereby creating a hazardous condition.

Study Session 6

Topic: Category I Appliance Flue Lining Systems
Reference: IFGC 501.13
Category: Chimneys and Vents
Subject: General Requirements

Code Text: *Flue lining systems for use with Category I appliances shall be limited to the following:*

1. *Flue lining systems complying with Section 501.12.*
2. *Chimney lining systems listed and labeled for use with gas appliances with draft hoods and other Category I gas appliances listed and labeled for use with Type B vents.*

Discussion and Commentary: For venting of Category I appliances, masonry chimneys are permitted to be used as a chase to install listed venting systems to remove products of combustion to the outdoors. Vent manufacturers supply listed kits or assemblies that provide a complete lining system for this purpose, including the vent material, supports and vent caps. Masonry chimneys with a clay flue lining complying with ASTM C315 are also approved for venting Category I appliances.

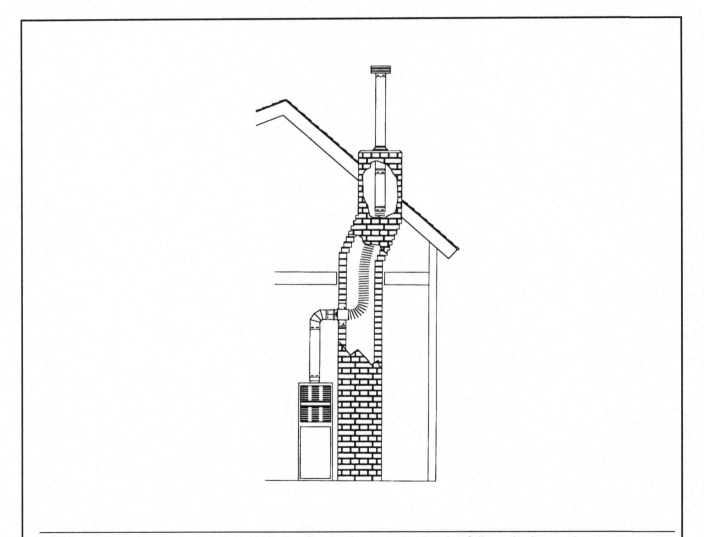

The appliance manufacturer's installation instructions must also be followed when using a masonry chimney with a flue lining as a vent.

Topic: Category II, III and IV Appliance Venting Systems
Reference: IFGC 501.14
Category: Chimneys and Vents
Subject: General Requirements

Code Text: *The design, sizing and installation of vents for Category II, III and IV appliances shall be in accordance with the appliance manufacturer's instructions.*

Discussion and Commentary: Category II, III and IV appliances may require a specialized type of venting system because of flue gas temperatures, operation efficiency or positive pressures. The manufacturer's installation instructions best address the specific venting requirements for the particular appliance.

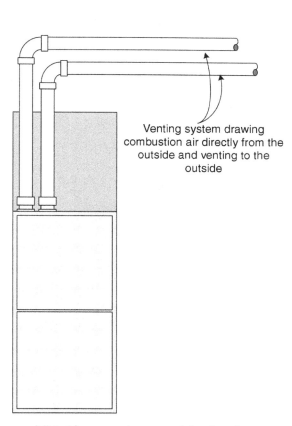

Venting system drawing combustion air directly from the outside and venting to the outside

A listed furnace using a specialized venting system, utilizing plastic pipe commonly used in the plumbing industry.

Venting requirements for Category II, III and IV appliances are not specifically addressed by the code. These specialized systems must be installed as specified by the appliance manufacturer.

Topic: Insulation Shield
Reference: IFGC 502.4

Category: Chimneys and Vents
Subject: Vents

Code Text: *Where vents pass through insulated assemblies, an insulation shield constructed of steel having a minimum thickness of 0.0187 inch (0.4712 mm) (No. 26 gage) shall be installed to provide clearance between the vent and the insulation material. The clearance shall not be less than the clearance to combustibles specified by the vent manufacturer's installation instructions. Where vents pass through attic space, the shield shall terminate not less than 2 inches (51 mm) above the insulation materials and shall be secured in place to prevent displacement. Insulation shields provided as part of a listed vent system shall be installed in accordance with the manufacturer's instructions.*

Discussion and Commentary: The insulation shield provisions typically are encountered when a vent passes through an attic before terminating above the roof. Vent materials are listed for a minimum clearance to combustible materials, and the attic shield maintains those clearances. In this application, all insulation is considered combustible material. Extending the shield at least 2 inches above the insulation prevents loose insulation from falling into the space between the vent and the metal shield. It also prevents blown-in type insulation from falling into the uninsulated stud bay containing the vent below the attic space.

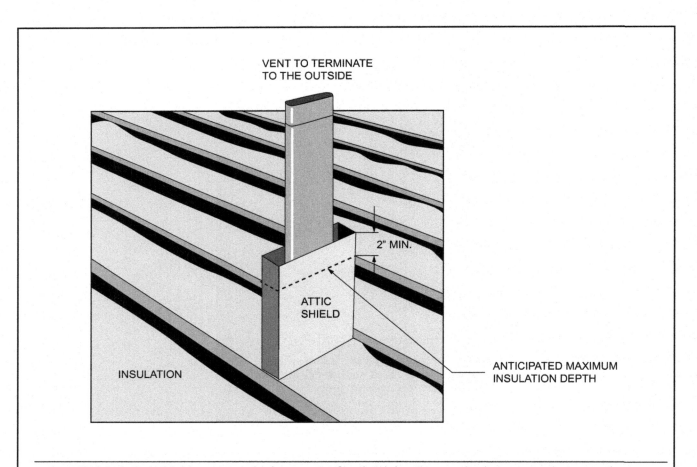

An attic insulation shield serves a dual purpose of maintaining the required clearance between the vent and combustibles, and of retaining loose insulation in place as intended to maintain the thermal envelope of the building.

Topic: Protection Against Physical Damage
Reference: IFGC 502.7
Category: Chimneys and Vents
Subject: Vents

Code Text: *In concealed locations, where a vent is installed through holes or notches in studs, joists, rafters or similar members less than $1^1/_2$ inches (38 mm) from the nearest edge of the member, the vent shall be protected by shield plates. Protective steel shield plates having a minimum thickness of 0.0575 inch (1.463 mm) (No. 16 gage) shall cover the area of the vent where the member is notched or bored and shall extend a minimum of 4 inches (102 mm) above sole plates, below top plates and to each side of a stud, joist or rafter.*

Discussion and Commentary: Vents installed in walls or other concealed spaces are subject to penetration by nails or screws during the application of drywall, trim and other finish materials. The resulting physical damage could impair the function, efficiency or fire-resistant properties of the vent and in a worst case could result in leakage of flue gases into the building. To protect the vent from damage in concealed spaces, the code requires steel shield plates where the vent passes through structural members such as studs, plates, joists and rafters and the vent is less than $1^1/_2$ inches from the edge of the member.

Protection against physical damage

Shield plates must cover the areas where finish materials are fastened to the structure and the vent is most vulnerable to structural damage. For added protection, the shield plate must extend at least 4 inches beyond each side of a stud, joist or rafter, 4 inches above a bottom plate and 4 inches below a top plate.

Study Session 6

Topic: Above-Ceiling Air-Handling Spaces
Reference: IFGC 503.3.6
Category: Chimneys and Vents
Subject: Venting Appliances

Code Text: *Where a venting system passes through an above-ceiling air-handling space or other non-ducted portion of an air-handling system, the venting system shall conform to one of the following requirements: (1) The venting system shall be a listed special gas vent; other venting system serving a Category III or Category IV appliance; or other positive pressure vent, with joints sealed in accordance with the appliance or vent manufacturer's instructions; (2) The venting system shall be installed such that fittings and joints between sections are not installed in the above-ceiling space, (3) The venting system shall be installed in a conduit or enclosure with sealed joints separating the interior of the conduit or enclosure from the ceiling space.*

Discussion and Commentary: The primary concern for venting systems that pass through concealed spaces used as return air plenums is that any products of combustion that leak into the plenum space will be circulated throughout the building. The code intends to provide added protection against such leakage by requiring vents meet one of three conditions. Special listed vents, vents with sealed joints and vents installed such that no joints occur in the plenum significantly reduce the possibility of any leakage into the plenum space and are acceptable for this installation. Otherwise, the vent must be isolated from the plenum space by being placed in a sealed conduit or enclosure.

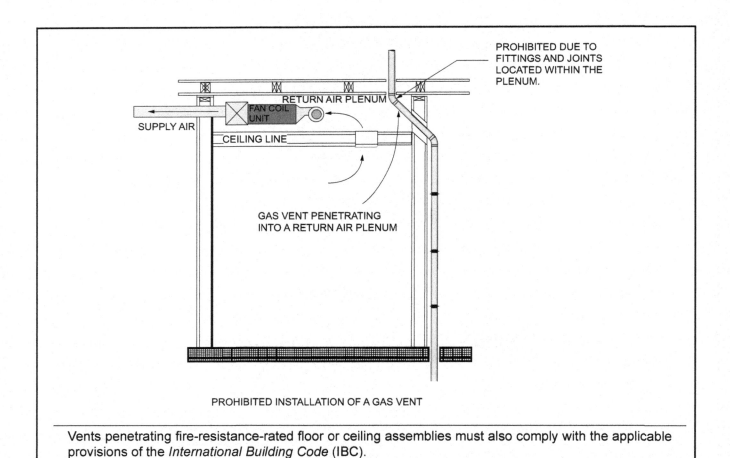

PROHIBITED INSTALLATION OF A GAS VENT

Vents penetrating fire-resistance-rated floor or ceiling assemblies must also comply with the applicable provisions of the *International Building Code* (IBC).

Topic: Plastic Piping
Reference: IFGC 503.4.1

Category: Chimneys and Vents
Subject: Venting of Appliances

Code Text: *Where plastic piping is used to vent an appliance, the appliance shall be listed for use with such venting materials and the appliance manufacturer's installation instructions shall identify the specific plastic piping material. The plastic pipe venting materials shall be labeled in accordance with the product standards specified by the appliance manufacturer or shall be listed and labeled in accordance with UL 1738. Plastic pipe and fittings used to vent appliances shall be installed in accordance with the appliance manufacturer's instructions. Plastic pipe venting materials listed and labeled in accordance with UL 1738 shall be installed in accordance with the vent manufacturer's instructions. Where a primer is required, it shall be of a contrasting color.*

Discussion and Commentary: Plastic piping formulated from PVC, CPVC or ABS is commonly used for venting of high-efficiency appliances with low flue-gas temperatures. Plastic piping is not listed as vent piping, but it performs well in these applications and is approved for venting when included in the appliance listing. Category III and IV appliances require a specialized venting system because of high efficiency operation, low temperature flue gases, production of condensate or positive pressure venting system. Plastic piping may be specified for some of these appliances, but for others it may not meet the criteria of the manufacturer.

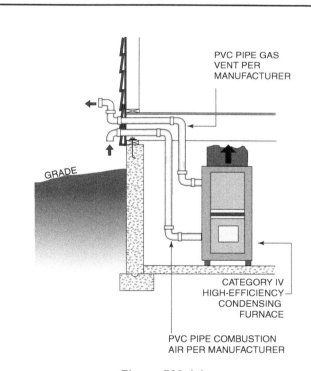

Figure 503.4.1
DIRECT-VENT APPLIANCE

Installation of plastic piping used to vent appliances must conform to the appliance manufacturer's installation instructions, including the priming and solvent cementing of joints.

Topic: Factory-Built Chimneys
Reference: IFGC 503.5.1
Category: Chimneys and Vents
Subject: Venting of Appliances

Code Text: *Factory-built chimneys shall be listed in accordance with UL 103. Factory-built chimneys used to vent appliances that operate at a positive vent pressure shall be listed for such application.*

Discussion and Commentary: Chimneys differ from vents in that they are designed to vent much higher temperature flue gases. Prefabricated chimneys typically have multiple walls and are insulated or air cooled. Factory built chimney systems must be listed and labeled by an approved testing agency. The label information contains the necessary minimum clearance to combustibles and the type of appliance the chimney has been tested for. Assembly and installation must follow the manufacturer's installation instructions.

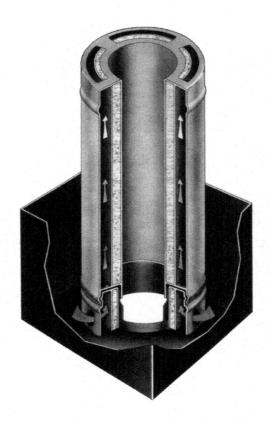

The IBC regulates the construction of masonry fireplaces and masonry chimneys.

Topic: Gas Vent Terminations
Reference: IFGC 503.6.5
Category: Chimneys and Vents
Subject: Venting of Appliances

Code Text: *A gas vent shall terminate in accordance with one of the following: (1) Gas vents that are 12 inches (305 mm) or less in size and located not less than 8 feet (2438 mm) from a vertical wall or similar obstruction shall terminate above the roof in accordance with Figure 503.6.4, (2) Gas vents that are over 12 inches (305 mm) in size or are located less than 8 feet (2438 mm) from a vertical wall or similar obstruction shall terminate not less than 2 feet (610 mm) above the highest point where they pass through the roof and not less than 2 feet (610 mm) above any portion of a building within 10 feet (3048 mm) horizontally. Additional Items 3 through 7 reference the applicable code sections for industrial appliances, direct-vent systems, appliances with integral vents, mechanical draft systems and ventilating hoods.*

Discussion and Commentary: Proper vent termination clearances promote the safe operation of an appliance and ensure that products of combustion are safely exhausted to the outside atmosphere. If the vent termination is not high enough above the roof surface, wind may prevent the vent from drawing properly and may create a downdraft, spilling products of combustion into the building. If the vent system is too high and exposed to the outside air, the flue gases may cool prematurely, causing condensation within the vent, resulting in corrosion and deterioration of the material.

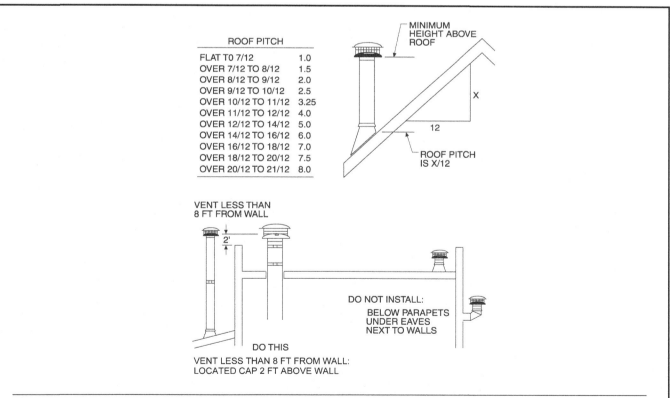

For vents that are 12 inches or less in size and terminate at least 8 feet from a vertical wall, Figure 503.6.5 provides the minimum termination distance above the roof based on roof slope. The distance is measured from the high side of the roof at the vent penetration to the lowest discharge opening.

Topic: Decorative Shrouds

Category: Chimneys and Vents

Reference: IFGC 503.6.5.1

Subject: Venting of Appliances

Code Text: *Decorative shrouds shall not be installed at the termination of gas vents except where such shrouds are listed for use with the specific gas venting system and are installed in accordance with manufacturer's installation instructions.*

Discussion and Commentary: Decorative shrouds are popular for architectural purposes to keep vent pipes out of sight. Shrouds are approved for installation when they are listed by an approved testing agency as compatible with the type of venting system being used. The listing of the appliance may also include installation with a particular type of decorative shroud.

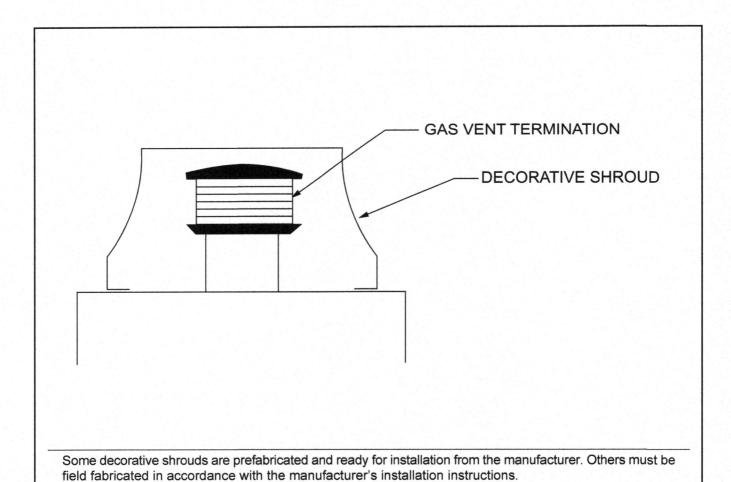

Some decorative shrouds are prefabricated and ready for installation from the manufacturer. Others must be field fabricated in accordance with the manufacturer's installation instructions.

Topic: Minimum Height
Reference: IFGC 503.6.6
Category: Chimneys and Vents
Subject: Venting of Appliances

Code Text: *A Type B or L gas vent shall terminate at least 5 feet (1524 mm) in vertical height above the highest connected appliance draft hood or flue collar. A Type B-W gas vent shall terminate at least 12 feet (3658 mm) in vertical height above the bottom of the wall furnace.*

Discussion and Commentary: The minimum height requirement ensures that there is adequate vertical rise for proper drafting of the appliance flue gases.

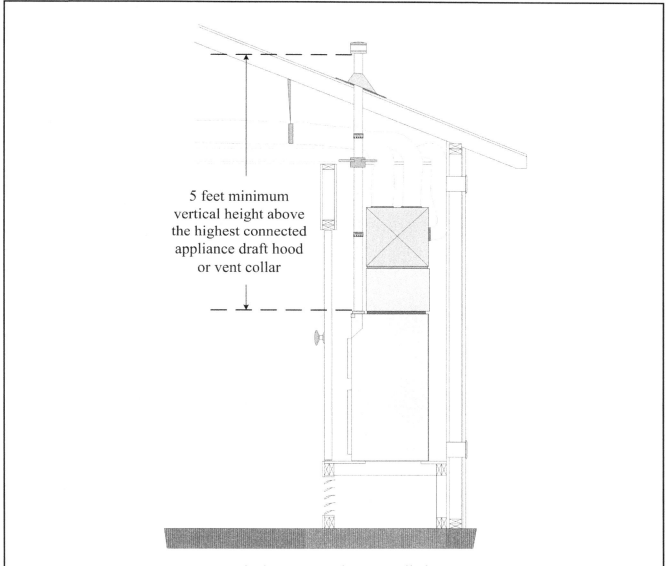

Forced Air Furnace Closet Installation

Minimum height requirements may also be covered in the appliance manufacturer's installation instructions and may exceed the requirements in the code, in which case the manufacturer's information prevails, so as to satisfy both requirements.

Topic: Category I Appliances
Reference: IFGC 503.6.10.1
Category: Chimneys and Vents
Subject: Venting of Appliances

Code Text: *The sizing of natural draft venting systems serving one or more listed appliances equipped with a draft hood or appliances listed for use with Type B gas vent, installed in a single story of a building, shall be in accordance with one of the following methods:* The methods include: *(1) The provisions of Section 504; (2) For sizing an individual gas vent for a single, draft-hood-equipped appliance, the effective area of the vent connector and the gas vent shall be not less than the area of the appliance draft hood outlet, nor greater than seven times the draft hood outlet area; (3) For sizing a gas vent connected to two appliances with draft hoods, the effective area of the vent shall be not less than the area of the larger draft hood outlet plus 50 percent of the area of the smaller draft hood outlet, nor greater than seven times the smaller draft hood outlet area;* and *(4) Engineering methods.*

Discussion and Commentary: Category I appliances operate with a nonpositive vent static pressure and with a flue-gas temperature that does not produce condensation in the vent. Section 503.6.10.1 only applies to sizing the vent system of Category I appliances that serve one story and have a natural draft venting system. This section does not intend to apply to fan-assisted appliances, which are covered in Section 504. The code provides four options for sizing the vent system, given the above scope. The most common method for sizing venting systems for modern Category I appliances utilizes Section 504. In practice, Items 2 and 3 have limited application for simple venting installations.

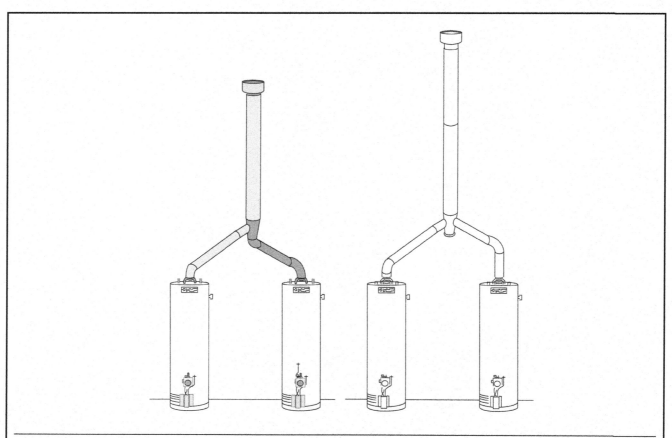

Depending on the appliance and the venting configuration, the appliance manufacturer's installation instructions may vary from the methods in Items 2 and 3 of Section 503.6.10.1 and be more in line with Section 504.

Topic: Support of Gas Vents
Reference: IFGC 503.6.12
Category: Chimneys and Vents
Subject: Venting of Applications

Code Text: *Gas vents shall be supported and spaced in accordance with the manufacturer's installation instructions.*

Discussion and Commentary: Adequate support of gas vents are specified by the vent manufacturer. Improper support may result in damage to fittings and draft hoods that are not designed to bear the weight of the venting system. Field-fabricated supports are not listed but are acceptable as a means of supporting the venting system, provided they comply with the manufacturer's installation instructions.

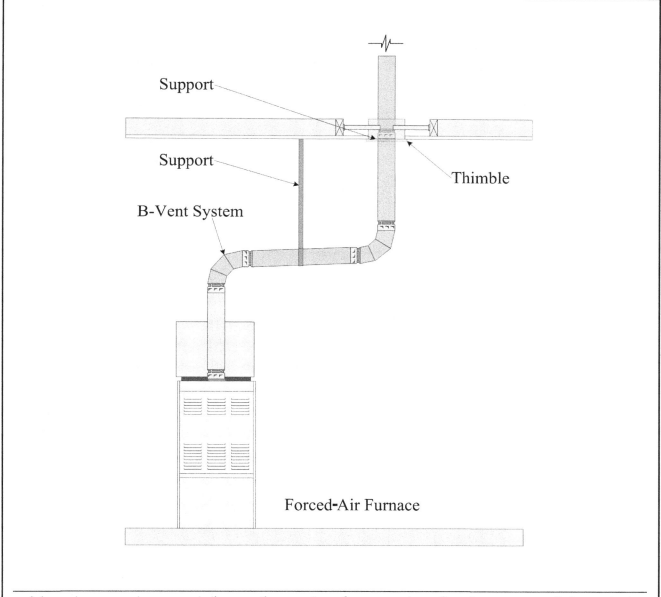

Adequate supports prevent the venting system from sagging. Sagging can result in a duct obstruction, which limits air movement.

Topic: Marking
Reference: IFGC 503.6.13

Category: Chimneys and Vents
Subject: Venting of Appliances

Code Text: *In those localities where solid and liquid fuels are used extensively, gas vents shall be permanently identified by a label attached to the wall or ceiling at a point where the vent connector enters the gas vent. The determination of where such localities exist shall be made by the code official. The label shall read:*

"This gas vent is for appliances that burn gas. Do not connect to solid or liquid fuel-burning appliances or incinerators."

Discussion and Commentary: Type B gas vents are designed and constructed to vent gas-fired appliances only. Connecting a solid or liquid-fueled appliance to a Type B vent would create an unsafe condition because the aluminum inner wall will not resist corrosive flue gas or higher temperatures generated by solid fuel or fuel oil combustion. The IFGC directs the code official to determine if marking the venting system is necessary based on the likelihood of a solid or liquid fueled appliance being mistakenly connected to an existing gas vent. The code official is best able to make this determination based on their knowledge of appliance installations.

This gas vent is for appliances that burn natural gas. Do not connect to solid or liquid fuel-burning appliances or incinerators.

When required, the warning sign must be placed in a conspicuous location on the wall or ceiling where the vent connector enters the gas vent.

Topic: Fastener Penetrations
Reference: IFGC 503.6.14
Category: Chimneys and Vents
Subject: Venting of Appliances

Code Text: *Screws, rivets and other fasteners shall not penetrate the inner wall of double-wall gas vents, except at the transition from an appliance draft hood outlet, a flue collar or a single-wall metal connector to a double-wall vent.*

Discussion and Commentary: Connections and fasteners for listed vents must be in accordance with the manufacturer's installation instructions. On Type B vents, for example, the fasteners utilize snap locks on the ends of the vent pipe or fittings. No other type of fastener is permitted on a Type B vent system unless specifically listed for that use. Screws that penetrate the inner liner of a Type B vent may impair the safe and effective venting of flue gases and decrease the durability and service life of the vent system.

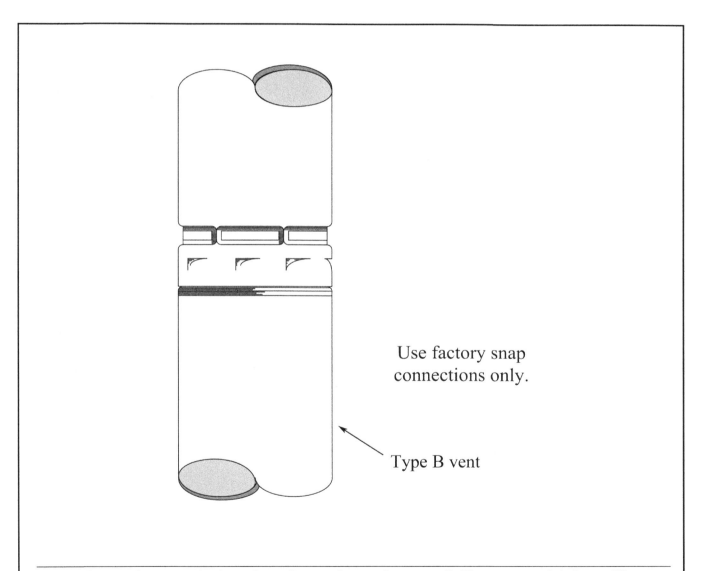

Type B vents have an aluminum inner liner and a steel outer wall. The two materials have different expansion. Screws, rivets or other fasteners that penetrate the inner liner may cause damage to the vent opening because the aluminum can expand and contract more than steel.

Study Session 6
IFGC Sections 501 through 503.6.14

1. Masonry chimneys shall be constructed in accordance with the _____.

    a. *International Fire Code* (IFC)

    b. *International Building Code* (IBC)

    c. *International Mechanical Code* (IMC)

    d. *International Residential Code* (IRC)

    Reference _____

2. Factory-built chimneys and vents for solid fuel appliances are regulated by the _____.

    a. *International Fire Code* (IFC)

    b. *International Building Code* (IBC)

    c. *International Mechanical Code* (IMC)

    d. *International Fuel Gas Code* (IFGC)

    Reference _____

3. An appliance shall not be connected to a flue serving a factory built fireplace unless the appliance is _____ for such an installation.

    a. listed
    b. manufactured
    c. designed
    d. equipped

    Reference _____

4. For a direct-vent fireplace with a sidewall vent, the vent termination must be a minimum of _____ inches from the swing of a door.
   a. 12
   b. 18
   c. 24
   d. 6

   Reference _____

5. Gas appliance connections to a masonry chimney flue must be at a point not less than _____ inches above the lowest portion of the interior of the chimney flue.
   a. 6
   b. 24
   c. 18
   d. 12

   Reference _____

6. Appliance connections to a chimney or vent equipped with a power exhauster shall be made on the _____ side of the exhauster.
   a. outlet
   b. inlet
   c. positive
   d. discharge

   Reference _____

7. Masonry chimney flues shall be provided with a cleanout opening having a minimum height of _____ inches.
   a. 4
   b. 6
   c. 8
   d. 10

   Reference _____

8. A listed unvented room heater does not require a vent when the aggregate input rating of all unvented appliances in the room does not exceed _____ Btu/h per cubic foot of the room volume.
   a. 20
   b. 25
   c. 30
   d. 40

   Reference_____

9. For vents passing through an attic, the attic insulation shield shall extend at least _____ inches above the insulation material.
   a. 6
   b. 12
   c. 2
   d. 4

   Reference _____

10. To protect vents in a concealed location from physical damage, steel shield plates shall have a minimum thickness of _____.

    a. No. 22 gage
    b. No. 16 gage
    c. No. 12 gage
    d. No 18 gage

    Reference _____

11. Vents passing through insulated assemblies require an insulation shield constructed of steel with a minimum thickness of _____.

    a. 0.0187 inch (No. 26 gage)
    b. 0.0236 inch (No. 24 gage)
    c. 0.0450 inch (No. 18 gage)
    d. 0.0575 inch (No. 16 gage)

    Reference _____

12. To prevent entry of room air into the flue, a _____ shall be provided below the point of connection of an appliance to the chimney flue serving a fireplace.

    a. noncombustible seal
    b. sheet metal collar
    c. means of access
    d. manual damper

    Reference_____

13. When a mechanical draft system serving an appliance is not performing, _____.

    a. an audible alarm shall sound
    b. power to the appliance shall be disconnected
    c. gas shall not flow to the main burners
    d. fan-assisted combustion shall operate

    Reference _____

14. Where double-wall vents are installed, fasteners shall _____.

    a. be spaced evenly around the vent
    b. not penetrate the inner wall.
    c. not be used at the transition from a flue collar
    d. be aluminum or stainless steel

    Reference _____

15. Termination for chimneys serving residential type or low heat appliances shall extend at least _____ feet above the highest point where they pass through a roof of a building.

    a. 2
    b. 3
    c. 5
    d. 7

    Reference_____

16. Given: A 12-inch diameter listed gas vent with a listed cap is located 9 feet from a vertical wall. The gas vent is being terminated outside a building that has a roof slope of 12/12. What is the minimum termination distance above the roof?

    a. 3.0 feet
    b. 3.25 feet
    c. 3.5 feet
    d. 4.0 feet

    Reference_____

17. Chimneys serving medium-heat appliances shall extend at least 10 feet higher than any portion of any building within _____ feet.

    a. 20
    b. 15
    c. 25
    d. 12

    Reference_____

18. Where required to protect vents from physical damage, protective shield plates shall extend a minimum of _____ inches above sole plates and below top plates.

    a. 4
    b. 2
    c. $3^1/_2$
    d. $1^1/_2$

    Reference_____

19. A Type L vent is permitted for_____.

    a. Category IV furnaces
    b. listed combination gas and solid fuel-burning appliances
    c. unlisted combination gas and oil-burning appliances
    d. listed combination gas and oil-burning appliances

    Reference_____

Study Session 6

20. A Type B or L vent shall terminate at least _____ feet in vertical height above the highest appliance draft hood or flue collar.

   a. 7
   b. 8
   c. 5
   d. 20

   Reference_____

21. On a roof with a 4/12 slope, an 8-inch Type B vent located 12 feet from a vertical wall shall terminate a minimum of _____ inches above the roof.

   a. 24
   b. 12
   c. 30
   d. 18

   Reference_____

22. Gas vents shall terminate not less than 3 feet above any forced air inlet located within _____ feet.

   a. 5
   b. 10
   c. 15
   d. 20

   Reference_____

23. Gas vents terminating less than 8 feet from a vertical wall shall terminate not less than _____ feet above any portion of a building within 10 feet.

   a. 2
   b. 3
   c. 5
   d. 6

   Reference_____

24. Decorative shrouds for gas vents shall be listed _____.

   a. as complying with UL 1738
   b. for use with the specific appliance
   c. for the specific gas venting system
   d. for use with gas vents

   Reference_____

25. A common gas vent serving appliances on more than one floor level shall be permitted for _____ appliances, provided that the venting system is designed and installed in accordance with approved engineering methods.

   a. Category I
   b. Category II
   c. Category III
   d. Category IV

   Reference_____

2021 IFGC Sections 503.7 through 506
Chimneys and Vents II

OBJECTIVE: To gain and understanding of the code provisions that minimize the hazards associated with the venting of combustion products, including the proper selection, design, construction and installation of chimneys and vents.

REFERENCE: Sections 503.7 through 506, 2021 *International Fuel Gas Code*

KEY POINTS:
- What determines the size of a common vent in a multistory vent system?
- What determines the diameter of the vent connector in a multistory installation?
- When should a gas vent be identified for the type of fuel being used?
- What are the restrictions when installing an uninsulated single wall vent in an outdoor location?
- What are the requirements for penetrating a roof of combustible material with a single wall vent?
- Are single wall vents permitted in concealed locations?
- What is the minimum distance between a direct vent termination and a window opening?
- When is a condensate disposal system required?
- Where is a vent connector required?
- What conditions apply to single wall vent connectors serving Category I appliances?
- How are minimum clearances from vent connectors to combustible material determined?
- When is a single wall vent connector permitted to penetrate a wall or floor?
- Where is a draft hood or barometric draft regulator permitted to be installed?
- Are manually operated dampers allowed to be installed in a vent connector?
- What precautions must be taken when adding elbows to a venting system?
- What restrictions apply to vents located outdoors when using the venting tables?

KEY POINTS:
(Cont'd)

- What is the optimum length of a vent connector?
- Under what conditions may the length of a vent connector be increased?
- What reductions apply to a common vertical vent when it is offset?
- How many 90-degree elbows are permitted in the common vent sizing tables?
- What reductions to the common vent capacity tables are required when elbows are added to the system?
- What material is permitted for construction of tee and wye fittings in a venting system?
- How is the total height of a common vent measured when serving multiple appliances located on the same floor?
- What rules apply to multistory common vents with offsets?
- How is the maximum flow area of a vent related to the flow area of the connected appliances?
- What are the requirements for venting commercial cooking appliances through a Type I or Type II hood?
- What temperatures determine if a factory built chimney is listed for building heating appliances or for medium-heat appliances?

Topic: Single-Wall Metal Pipe
Reference: IFGC 503.7
Category: Chimneys and Vents
Subject: Venting of Appliances

Code Text: *Single-wall metal pipe vents shall comply with Sections 503.7.1 through 503.7.13.*

Discussion and Commentary: Single-wall metal pipe is approved for use as gas vent pipe with several installation limitations and conditions. The provisions for single-wall metal pipe address specify the approved locations, length of run, clearance to combustibles, penetrations of combustible materials and potential condensation issues. For example, single-wall metal pipe is not permitted to originate in or to pass through any unoccupied or concealed space such as an attic or crawl space. The IFGC further restricts its use for runs directly from the space containing the appliance to the outdoors through a roof or exterior wall. Listed appliance manufacturers typically specify a listed venting system such as Type B gas vent for their appliances or specialized venting systems such as plastic pipe venting for high efficiency equipment.

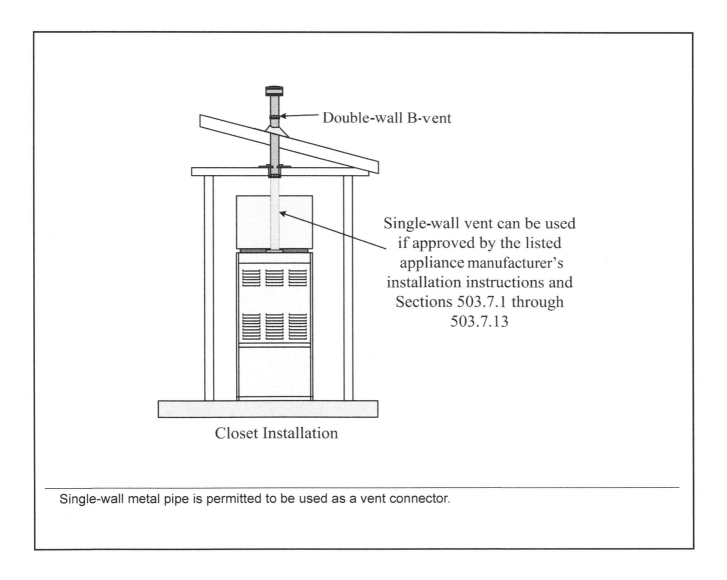

Closet Installation

Single-wall metal pipe is permitted to be used as a vent connector.

Topic: Venting Termination

Category: Chimneys and Vents

Reference: IFGC 503.8

Subject: Venting of Appliances

Code Text: *The clearances for through-the-wall direct-vent terminals and nondirect-vent terminals shall be in accordance with Table 503.8 and Figure 503.8.*

Discussion and Commentary: The code sets minimum clearances for through-the-wall, direct-vent terminals to prevent flue gases from entering the building. The minimum dimension from the termination to any opening into the building is based on the input rating of the direct-vent appliance as indicated in Table 503.8. Minimum ground clearance is set at 12 inches to ensure proper operation of the vent system. These values in the code are minimums and the clearances set by the manufacturer of the appliance must also be followed. Table 503.8 corresponds with Figure 503.8, showing where venting systems are permitted to terminate. In accordance with the exception, the clearances in Table 503.8 do not apply to the combustion air intake of a direct-vent appliance.

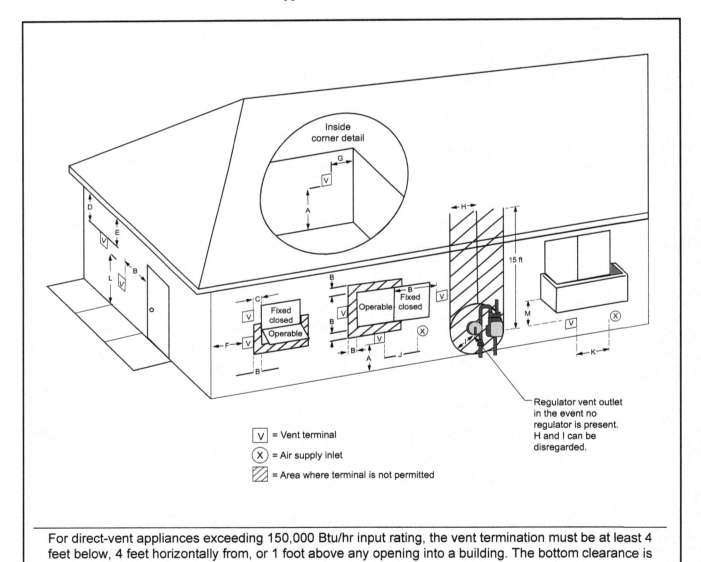

For direct-vent appliances exceeding 150,000 Btu/hr input rating, the vent termination must be at least 4 feet below, 4 feet horizontally from, or 1 foot above any opening into a building. The bottom clearance is at least 12 inches above grade.

Topic: Venting System Termination Location **Category:** Chimneys and Vents
Reference: Table 503.8, Figure Clearance L **Subject:** Venting Appliances

Code Text: *Clearance above paved sidewalk or paved driveway located on public property. Minimum Clearance for Direct-Vent Terminals: 7 feet and shall not be located above public walkways or other areas where condensate or vapor can cause a nuisance or hazard.*

Discussion and Commentary: Venting systems of condensate producing appliances are not permitted to terminate through the wall at a location over public walkways. Condensate discharging at these locations has the potential for creating hazards such as ice buildup or slippery walking surfaces. The IFGC also prohibits through-the-wall venting terminations where condensate would create a nuisance or be detrimental to the operation of equipment. For example, freezing condensate may cause the obstruction of regulators or relief valve openings.

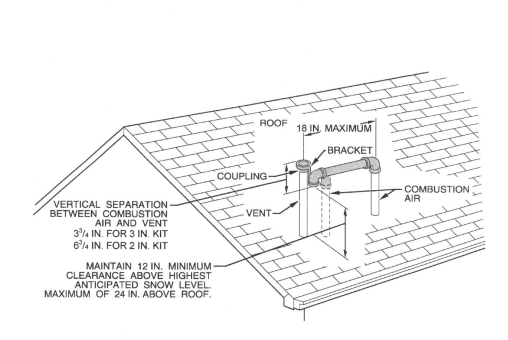

Example of manufacturer's details for direct-vent appliance terminals

The manufacturer's installation instructions also restrict the vent termination location and specify other installation requirements for the venting system of condensing appliances.

Topic: Vent Connectors Located in Unconditioned Areas
Reference: IFGC 503.10.2.2
Category: Chimneys and Vents
Subject: Venting of Appliances

Code Text: *Where the vent connector used for an appliance having a draft hood or a Category I appliance is located in or passes through attics, crawl spaces or other unconditioned spaces, that portion of the vent connector shall be listed Type B, Type L or listed vent material having equivalent insulation properties.* See the exception.

Discussion and Commentary: In cold climates, the installation of a single-wall vent pipe or connector in an attic, a crawl space or another unconditioned space can cause moisture to condense in the vent because of temperature differences between the flue gas and the vent. Formation of this condensate will result in deterioration and eventual failure of the vent. To remedy this problem, an insulated type vent, such as a Type B or Type L vent is required for connectors in unconditioned locations. The exception for certain climates permits a single-wall connector to be enclosed in an exterior wall of unconditioned areas other than crawl spaces or attics.

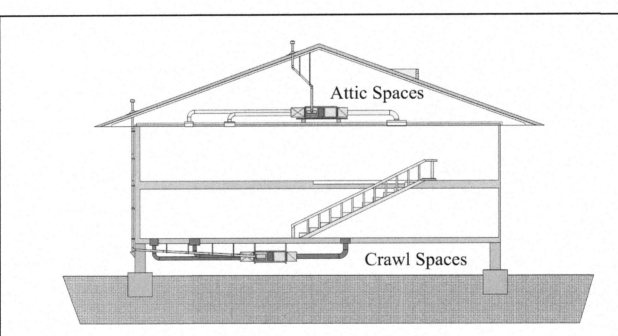

Vent connectors for Category 1 appliances located in unconditioned attics or crawl spaces shall be listed Type B, Type L or listed vent material having equivalent insulation properties.

With today's emphasis on higher efficiency appliances and energy conservation practices, single wall vent pipe is rarely installed as a venting system. In addition to condensation issues and minimum clearances to combustibles, single wall pipe loses heat very quickly and is significantly limited in application.

Topic: Vent Connectors Clearances
Reference: IFGC 503.10.5
Category: Chimneys and Vents
Subject: Venting of Appliances

Code Text: *Minimum clearances from vent connectors to combustible material shall be in accordance with Table 503.10.5. See the exception for reduced clearances in accordance with Table 308.2.*

Discussion and Commentary: One drawback of single-wall metal pipe vent connectors is the greater distance required between combustibles and the vent connector, which ranges from 6 inches for listed residential appliances with draft hoods to 36 inches for medium-heat appliances. Conversely, listed Type B vent connectors typically require a 1-inch clearance for residential appliances listed for use with Type B vents. Similarly, listed factory-built chimneys require significantly less clearance to combustibles than single-wall pipe. The clearances for single-wall metal connectors are permitted to be reduced with the prescribed methods for protecting combustible materials. The vent connector provisions in Section 503.10.5 apply to Category I appliances.

TABLE 503.10.5
CLEARANCES FOR CONNECTORS[a]

APPLIANCE	MINIMUM DISTANCE FROM COMBUSTIBLE MATERIAL			
	Listed Type B gas vent material	Listed Type L vent material	Single-wall metal pipe	Factory-built chimney sections
Listed appliances with draft hoods and appliances listed for use with Type B gas vents	As listed	As listed	6 inches	As listed
Residential boilers and furnaces with listed gas conversion burner and with draft hood	6 inches	6 inches	9 inches	As listed
Residential appliances listed for use with Type L vents	Not permitted	As listed	9 inches	As listed
Listed gas-fired toilets	Not permitted	As listed	As listed	As listed
Unlisted residential appliances with draft hood	Not permitted	6 inches	9 inches	As listed
Residential and low-heat appliances other than above	Not permitted	9 inches	18 inches	As listed
Medium-heat appliances	Not permitted	Not permitted	36 inches	As listed

For SI: 1 inch = 25.4 mm.

a. These clearances shall apply unless the manufacturer's installation instructions for a listed appliance or connector specify different clearances, in which case the listed clearances shall apply.

The primary consideration for minimum clearances to combustibles is the surface temperature of the vent connector. The clearance must be sufficient to prevent possible ignition of the combustible materials.

Topic: Vent Connector Length
Reference: IFGC 503.10.9
Category: Chimneys and Vents
Subject: Venting Appliances

Code Text: *The maximum horizontal length of a single-wall connector shall be 75 percent of the height of the chimney or vent except for engineered systems. The maximum horizontal length of a Type B double-wall connector shall be 100 percent of the height of the chimney or vent except for engineered systems.*

Discussion and Commentary: A single-wall connector is restricted to a maximum length that is 25 percent less than a Type B connector on the same appliance. Listed Type B vent connectors are insulated and have the capacity to retain more heat inside the vent than single wall connectors. With more heat retained in the vent, the draw on double wall vent pipe is greater than occurs with single wall pipe.

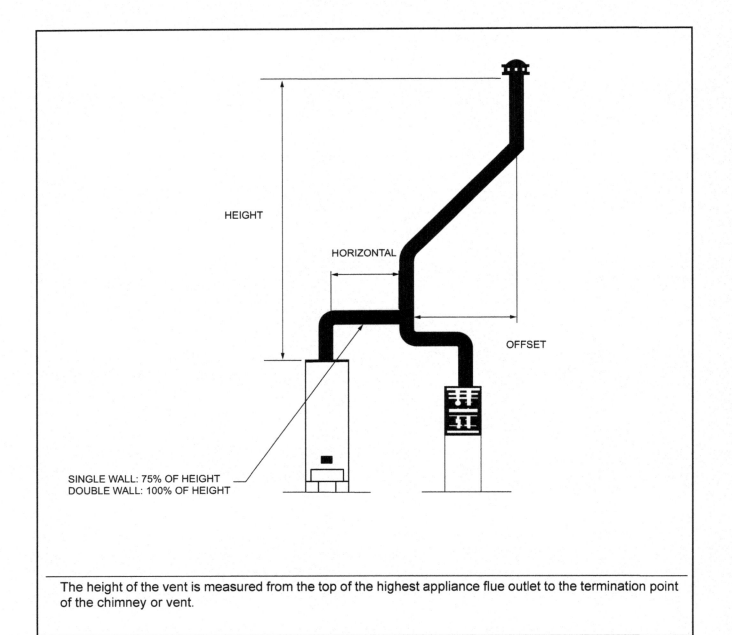

The height of the vent is measured from the top of the highest appliance flue outlet to the termination point of the chimney or vent.

| Topic: Draft Hood Location | Category: Chimneys and Vents |
| Reference: IFGC 503.12.5 | Subject: Venting of Appliances |

Code Text: *Draft hoods and barometric draft regulators shall be installed in the same room or enclosure as the appliance in such a manner as to prevent any difference in pressure between the hood or regulator and the combustion air supply.*

Discussion and Commentary: Draft control devices (e.g., draft hoods and barometric dampers) function to maintain a constant draft through the appliance combustion chamber and the venting system to provide efficient operation and proper exhaust of combustion products. To operate properly, draft control devices must be located in the same room as the appliance so that the ambient pressure is equal.

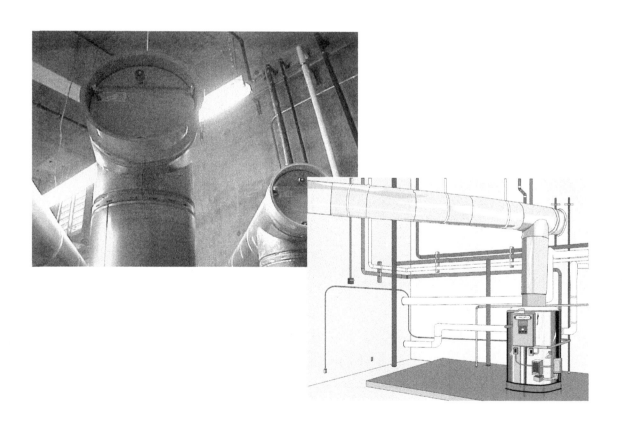

Draft hoods and barometric dampers introduce cooler ambient air into the venting system that improves drafting of the system and reduces the temperature of the vent system.

Topic: Vent Offsets
Reference: IFGC 504.2.3
Category: Chimneys and Vents
Subject: Sizing of Category 1 Appliance Venting Systems

Code Text: *Single-appliance venting configurations with zero (0) lateral lengths in Tables 504.2(1), 504.2(2) and 504.2(5) shall not have elbows in the venting system. Single-appliance venting configurations with lateral lengths include two 90-degree (1.57 rad) elbows. For each additional elbow up to and including 45 degrees (0.79 rad), the maximum capacity listed in the venting tables shall be reduced by 5 percent. For each additional elbow greater than 45 degrees (0.79 rad) up to and including 90 degrees (1.57 rad), the maximum capacity listed in the venting tables shall be reduced by 10 percent. Where multiple offsets occur in a vent, the total lateral length of all offsets combined shall not exceed that specified in Tables 504.2(1) through 504.2(5).*

Discussion and Commentary: Vertical vents with no elbows (zero lateral length) have the least resistance to flow. Offsets created by elbows significantly increase the resistance to flow and reduce the capacity of the venting system. The sizing tables account for two elbows for creating offsets of varying lengths. Vents that are using in excess of two 90-degree elbows require that 10 percent be subtracted from the capacity listed in the venting tables for each additional elbow. If the elbow is not greater than 45 degrees, then a 5 percent reduction per additional elbow is taken from the values in the tables.

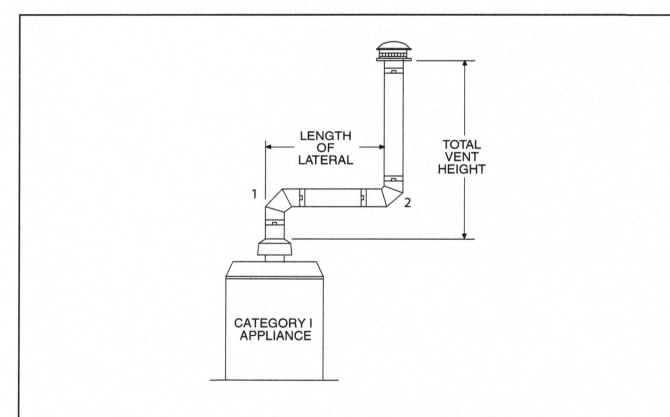

In addition to reducing resistance to flow, minimizing offsets in an attic area is preferable because it provides less surface area to cool down vent gases resulting in better drafting. However, for aesthetic reasons, a through-the roof vent termination typically is not desirable on the street side of the building, and offsets are often necessary to place the vent termination on the back side of the building. The first two 90 degree angles, as shown, are already accounted for in Tables 504.2(1), 504.2(2) and 504.2(5) where a lateral length is present.

Topic: Commercial Cooking Appliances
Reference: IFGC 505.1.1
Category: Chimneys and Vents
Subject: Exhaust Hood Venting

Code Text: *Where commercial cooking appliances are vented by means of the Type I or II kitchen exhaust hood system that serves such appliances, the exhaust system shall be fan powered and the appliances shall be interlocked with the exhaust hood system to prevent appliance operation when the exhaust hood system is not operating. The method of interlock between the exhaust hood system and the appliances equipped with standing pilot burner ignition systems shall not cause such pilots to be extinguished. Where a solenoid valve is installed in the gas piping as part of an interlock system, gas piping shall not be installed to bypass such valve. Dampers shall not be installed in the exhaust system.* See the exception to an interlock system that permits heat sensors or other approved methods to automatically activate the exhaust hood system when cooking operations occur.

Discussion and Commentary: In addition to exhausting steam, smoke and grease laden vapors produced by cooking activities, Type I or II hood systems also usually serve as the gas vent for the commercial cooking appliances. The appliances are not permitted to operate without the hood in operation—that is, the appliances and hood system must be interlocked. If the hood is disabled or not working for any reason, the appliances are unable to operate.

Exhaust Hood Interlock with Cooking Appliance (Solenoid Gas Valve)

Additional requirements for commercial exhaust hoods are found in the *International Mechanical Code* (IMC). The IMC and IFGC have identical safety requirements for an interlock system, heat sensors or other approved methods to ensure that the exhaust fans are operating whenever the cooking appliances are in operation.

Topic: Building Heating Appliances
Reference: IFGC 506.1
Category: Chimneys and Vents
Subject: Factory-Built Chimneys

Code Text: *Factory-built chimneys for building heating appliances producing flue gases having a temperature not greater than 1,000°F (538°C), measured at the entrance to the chimney, shall be listed and labeled in accordance with UL 103 and shall be installed and terminated in accordance with the manufacturer's installation instructions.*

Discussion and Commentary: Factory-built chimneys may be double-wall or triple-wall assemblies and are constructed similarly to a double-wall Type B vent. The major difference is that a Type B vent is constructed with a steel outer shell and an aluminum liner, whereas the factory-built chimney has a steel outer shell and a stainless steel inner liner. The stainless steel liner is capable of withstanding much greater temperatures. Sizing and installation of factory-built chimneys are governed by the manufacturer's installation instructions.

Venting systems for building heating appliances are capable of handling flue gases up to 1,000°F. Venting systems for medium-heat appliances are rated for flue-gas temperatures over 1,000°F.

Quiz

Study Session 7
IFGC Sections 503.7 through 506

1. Which of the following is a code compliant clearance for a through-the-wall vent terminal from a mechanical air supply inlet? _____.

    a. 3 feet below

    b. 4 feet to the side

    c. 12 inches above

    d. 10 feet horizontally

    Reference _____

2. A single-wall metal pipe vent shall terminate at least _____ inches higher than any portion of a building within 10 feet horizontally.

    a. 24   b. 30

    c. 36   d. 42

    Reference _____

3. Which vent connector is not permitted in an uninsulated attic serving a Category I appliance? _____.

    a. Type B vent

    b. Type L vent

    c. Single-wall metal pipe

    d. other listed vent materials

    Reference _____

Study Session 7 143

4. Single-wall metal pipe vent shall be constructed of galvanized sheet steel not less than _____ in thickness.

   a. 0.0360 inch

   b. 0.0304 inch

   c. 0.0240 inch

   d. 0.0190 inch

   Reference _____

5. For single-wall metal pipe to be used outdoors for venting appliances, the 99-percent winter design temperature must not be less than _____ degrees Fahrenheit.

   a. 0   b. 32

   c. 40   d. 50

   Reference _____

6. A single-wall metal pipe vent shall terminate at least _____ feet in vertical height above the highest appliance draft hood outlet.

   a. 5   b. 10

   c. 15   d. 20

   Reference _____

7. When terminating above a roof, a single-wall metal pipe vent shall extend at least _____ above the highest point where it passes through the roof.

   a. 1 foot   b. 2 feet

   c. 3 feet   d. 4 feet

   Reference _____

8. Where a single-wall metal pipe vent passes through a roof constructed of combustible material, a noncombustible, nonventilating thimble shall extend at least _____ inches above and 6 inches below the roof.

   a. 12   b. 6

   c. 24   d. 18

   Reference _____

9. Single-wall metal pipe vent is permitted to pass through a(n) _____ constructed of combustible materials.

   a. inside wall b. attic
   c. floor d. exterior wall

   Reference _____

10. A mechanical draft venting system with an input value of 90,000 Btu/hr terminates through an exterior wall, directly above an operable window. The vent termination must be located a minimum of _____ above the window.

    a. 3 feet b. 4 feet
    c. 1 foot d. 2 feet

    Reference _____

11. The bottom of the vent terminal and air intake for a direct-vent appliance shall be located at least _____ inches above finished ground level.

    a. 6 b. 12
    c. 18 d. 24

    Reference _____

12. The vent terminal of a direct-vent appliance with an input of 20,000 Btu per hour shall be located at least _____ inches from any air opening into a building.

    a. 12 b. 18
    c. 6 d. 9

    Reference _____

13. In general, a vent connector for a Category I appliance shall slope upward toward the chimney or vent at least _____ inch per foot.

    a. $1/4$ b. $1/2$
    c. $1/8$ d. $3/8$

    Reference _____

14. The horizontal length of a single-wall connector shall be not greater than _____ percent of the height of the vent or chimney.

    a. 25
    b. 50
    c. 75
    d. 100

    Reference _____

15. The horizontal length of a Type B double-wall connector shall be not greater than _____ percent of the height of the vent or chimney.

    a. 25
    b. 50
    c. 75
    d. 100

    Reference _____

16. The minimum thickness required for a 16-inch diameter steel vent connector with an internal area of 190 square inches serving a medium-heat appliance is _____.

    a. 0.053 inch
    b. 0.067 inch
    c. 0.093 inch
    d. 0.123 inch

    Reference _____

17. Barometric draft regulators shall be installed in a manner to prevent any difference in pressure between the regulator and the _____ air supply.

    a. ambient
    b. combustion
    c. makeup
    d. ventilation

    Reference _____

18. For a residential furnace with a listed gas conversion burner and draft hood, a single-wall metal pipe connector requires a minimum clearance of _____ inches to combustible materials.

    a. 9
    b. 18
    c. 6
    d. 12

    Reference _____

19. Generally, the relief opening of a draft hood shall be located a minimum of _____ inches from any surface.

    a. 9   b. 12

    c. 3   d. 6

Reference_____

20. Vent connectors shall not be increased in size more than _____ size(s) greater than the draft hood outlet.

    a. 2   b. 3

    c. 4   d. 1

Reference_____

21. For a connector with two 90-degree elbows and two 45-degree elbows, the maximum capacity of the vent connector shall be reduced by _____ percent from the capacity listed in the common vent sizing tables for two or more appliances.

    a. 20   b. 15

    c. 10   d. 5

Reference_____

22. Where commercial cooking appliances are vented by means of a Type I or II kitchen hood, an interlock shall prevent the _____ from operating when the exhaust system is not operating.

    a. standing pilots   b. appliance

    c. hood fan   d. solenoid valve

Reference_____

23. The vent terminal of a direct-vent appliance with an input of 60,000 Btu/h shall be located at least _____ inches from any air opening into a building.

    a. 18   b. 6

    c. 9   d. 12

Reference_____

24. Generally, for vent systems serving more than one appliance, an 8-inch diameter connector is limited to a maximum horizontal length of _____ feet.

    a. 12   b. 9

    c. 6   d. 4

Reference_____

25. What is the minimum clearance required between a vent connector and combustible materials for an unlisted residential appliance with a draft hood served by a single-wall metal pipe vent?

    a. 6 inches   b. 9 inches

    c. 18 inches   d. 36 inches

Reference_____

2021 IFGC Sections 601 through 614
Specific Appliances I

OBJECTIVE: To develop an understanding of the code provisions for regulating specific appliances including heating, cooling, decorative, illuminating, cooking and industrial appliances.

REFERENCE: Sections 601 through 614, 2021 *International Fuel Gas Code*

KEY POINTS:
- What standards apply to decorative appliances?
- Vented gas fireplaces shall be tested in accordance with what standard?
- What restrictions are placed on wall furnaces installed between bathrooms and adjoining rooms?
- What is the minimum clearance distance between a swinging door and a wall heater inlet or outlet?
- When are ducts allowed to be installed on wall furnaces?
- What are the access requirements for wall furnaces?
- What are the clearance requirements for wall furnaces with a horizontal warm air outlet?
- What distances are required between the register on a floor furnace to draperies, doors and similar objects?
- Where should the location of a thermostat be in relation to the floor furnace?
- What code regulates the framework that supports a floor furnace?
- What is the minimum clearance between the lowest portion of a floor furnace and grade?
- Where are access panels required for ducted furnace installations?
- Where shall a duct furnace be located in relationship to a circulating air blower?
- What restrictions are placed on clothes dryer exhaust ducts related to connection with other systems?
- What provisions apply to fire dampers in relation to a dryer exhaust duct system?
- Where are dryer exhaust duct systems allowed to terminate?

KEY POINTS:
(Cont'd)

- What is make up air, and when is it required when installing a dryer exhaust system?
- What is the diameter mandated by the code for a dryer exhaust duct?
- What is the maximum distance between supports for dryer exhaust ducts?
- What restrictions apply to connections of dryer exhaust ducts?
- When can a dryer exhaust duct power ventilator be used, and how is the maximum duct length determined?
- What is the maximum distance a fastener can penetrate into a dryer exhaust duct at a joint?
- What is the maximum length for a transition duct in a dryer exhaust system?
- How is the maximum length of a dryer exhaust duct determined?
- What are the requirements for installing dryer exhaust systems in a common multi-story duct system?
- What is the minimum thickness and material for a duct in a dryer exhaust system?
- What clearances are required between commercial dryer exhaust ducts and combustible material?

Topic: Door Swing
Reference: IFGC 608.4
Category: Specific Appliances
Subject: Vented Wall Furnaces

Code Text: *Vented wall furnaces shall be located so that a door cannot swing within 12 inches (305 mm) of an air inlet or air outlet of such furnace measured at right angles to the opening. Doorstops or door closers shall not be installed to obtain this clearance.*

Discussion and Commentary: Prescribed clearances must be maintained adjacent to wall heaters to prevent ignition of combustible materials. The minimum 12-inch clearance provisions apply to doors in an open position. This clearance dimension for doors is measured at a right angle to the air inlet or outlet at the front of the wall furnace. Because doorstops and closures can be removed at any time, they are not considered satisfactory safeguards for maintaining the clearance to the door.

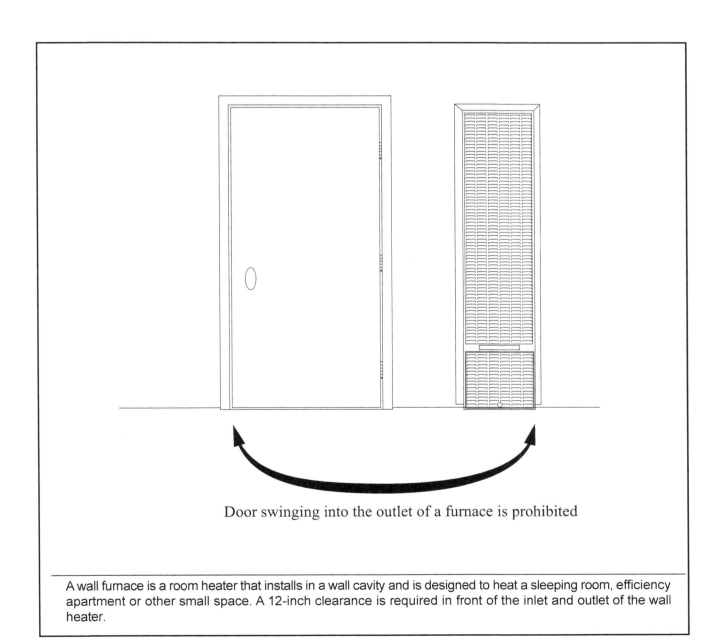

Door swinging into the outlet of a furnace is prohibited

A wall furnace is a room heater that installs in a wall cavity and is designed to heat a sleeping room, efficiency apartment or other small space. A 12-inch clearance is required in front of the inlet and outlet of the wall heater.

Topic: Ducts Prohibited
Reference: IFGC 608.5
Category: Specific Applications
Subject: Vented Wall Furnaces

Code Text: *Ducts shall not be attached to wall furnaces. Casing extension boots shall not be installed unless listed as part of the appliance.*

Discussion and Commentary: Wall heaters are designed to heat small spaces by discharging warm air directly into the space. Ducts are not approved for installation on wall heaters. The added resistance of air flow across the fire box surface may cause overheating resulting in a fire or burn hazard or damage to the appliance. Only extension boots that are specifically listed as part of the appliance are permitted. These are provided by the appliance manufacturer and are intended to improve heat distribution to the room.

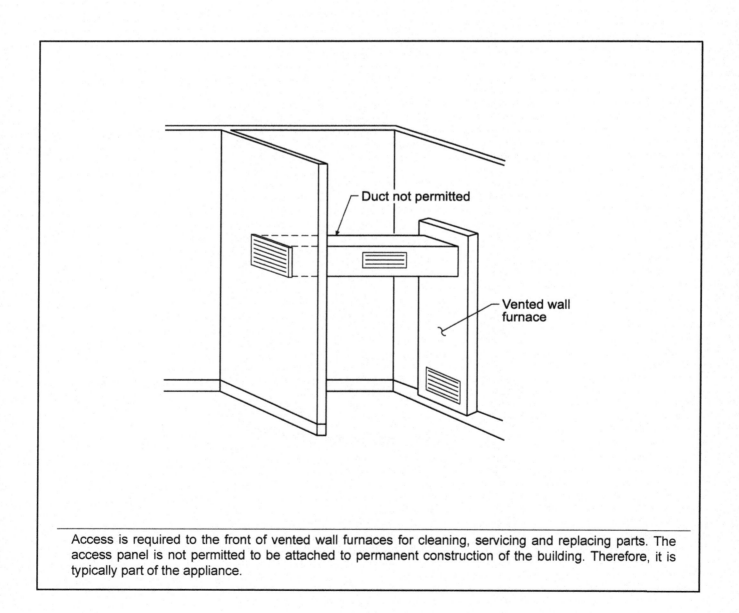

Access is required to the front of vented wall furnaces for cleaning, servicing and replacing parts. The access panel is not permitted to be attached to permanent construction of the building. Therefore, it is typically part of the appliance.

Topic: Placement
Reference: IFGC 609.2
Category: Specific Appliances
Subject: Floor Furnaces

Code Text: *The following provisions apply to floor furnaces:*

1. *Floors. Floor furnaces shall not be installed in the floor of any doorway, stairway landing, aisle or passageway of any enclosure, public or private, or in an exitway from any such room or space.*
2. *Walls and corners. The register of a floor furnace with a horizontal warm-air outlet shall not be placed closer than 6 inches (152 mm) to the nearest wall. A distance of at least 18 inches (457 mm) from two adjoining sides of the floor furnace register to walls shall be provided to eliminate the necessity of occupants walking over the warm-air discharge. The remaining sides shall be permitted to be placed not closer than 6 inches (152 mm) to a wall. Wall-register models shall not be placed closer than 6 inches (152 mm) to a corner.*
3. *Draperies. The furnace shall be placed so that a door, drapery or similar object cannot be nearer than 12 inches (305 mm) to any portion of the register of the furnace.*
4. *Floor construction. Floor furnaces shall not be installed in concrete floor construction built on grade.*
5. *Thermostat. The controlling thermostat for a floor furnace shall be located within the same room or space as the floor furnace or shall be located in an adjacent room or space that is permanently open to the room or space containing the floor furnace.*

Discussion and Commentary: Floor furnaces radiate warm air into the room through a register in the floor and typically are used for heating single rooms or small dwellings units. The register location requirements primarily address fire safety and protection of occupants from tripping hazards and accidental contact with hot surfaces. Required clearances from materials and furnishings are necessary to prevent potential ignition of combustible materials.

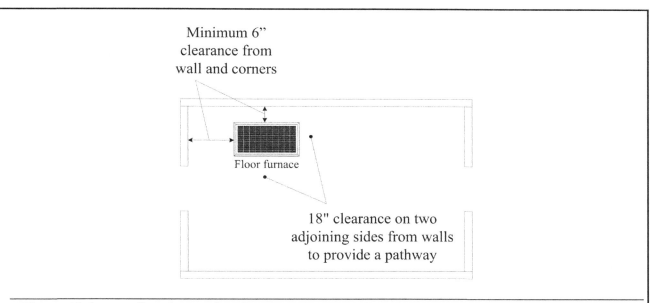

The restrictions on floor furnace locations intend to maintain a clear path for occupants without walking on the floor furnace warm air grille. The register is not permitted to be installed in the floor of any travel or exit route and must maintain at least 18 inches clearance on two sides between the floor furnace register and walls.

Topic: Clearance
Reference: IFGC 609.4
Category: Specific Appliances
Subject: Floor Furnaces

Code Text: *The lowest portion of the floor furnace shall have not less than a 6-inch (152 mm) clearance from the grade level; except where the lower 6-inch (152 mm) portion of the floor furnace is sealed by the manufacturer to prevent entrance of water, the minimum clearance shall be not less than 2 inches (51 mm). Where such clearances cannot be provided, the ground below and to the sides shall be excavated to form a pit under the furnace so that the required clearance is provided beneath the lowest portion of the furnace. A 12-inch (305 mm) minimum clearance shall be provided on all sides except the control side, which shall have an 18-inch (457 mm) minimum clearance.*

Discussion and Commentary: Clearances for the floor furnace prevent the cabinet and gas valve assembly from coming in contact with the ground or moisture, which would result in corrosion and damage to the appliance. The clearances also provide space for service, maintenance, repair and inspection when required.

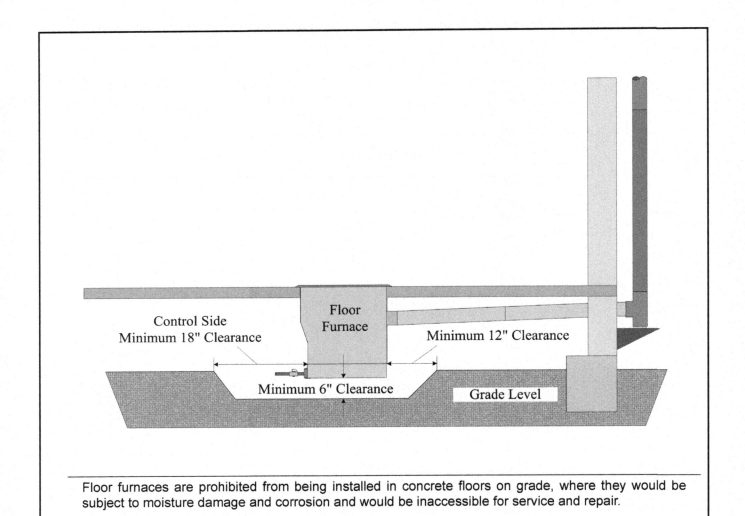

Floor furnaces are prohibited from being installed in concrete floors on grade, where they would be subject to moisture damage and corrosion and would be inaccessible for service and repair.

Topic: Installation
Reference: IFGC 614.1
Category: Specific Appliances
Subject: Clothes Dryer Exhaust

Code Text: *Clothes dryers shall be exhausted in accordance with the manufacturer's instructions. Dryer exhaust systems shall be independent of all other systems, shall convey the moisture and any products of combustion to the outside of the building.*

Discussion and Commentary: Exhaust systems for gas clothes dryers convey both moisture and products of combustion, which must be discharged directly to the outdoors. The location of the outdoor termination, including clearances to grade and any openings into the building, is determined by the manufacturer's installation instructions.

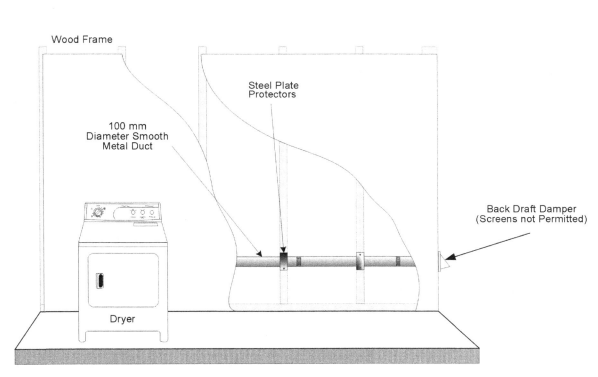

Dryer Exhaust System to Terminate to the Outside of the Building

Dryer ducts are considered an exhaust system rather than a venting system. Using Type B vents for a dryer exhaust system is not approved by the manufacturer or listing of the appliance, or the code. Sheet metal ductwork constructed of galvanized steel is approved and will effectively convey moisture and products of combustion to the outdoors if properly supported, fastened and sealed.

Topic: Exhaust Installation
Reference: IFGC 614.4
Category: Specific Appliances
Subject: Clothes Dryer Exhaust

Code Text: *Exhaust ducts for clothes dryers shall terminate on the outside of the building and shall be equipped with a backdraft damper. Screens shall not be installed at the duct termination. Ducts shall not be connected or installed with sheet metal screws or other fasteners that will obstruct the flow. Clothes dryer exhaust ducts shall not be connected to a vent connector, vent or chimney. Clothes dryer exhaust ducts shall not extend into or through ducts or plenums. Clothes dryer exhaust ducts shall be sealed in accordance with Section 603.9 of the* International Mechanical Code. *The passageway of dryer exhaust duct terminals shall be undiminished in size and shall provide an open area of not less than 12.5 square inches (8065 mm^2).*

Discussion and Commentary: Dryer exhaust systems require a backdraft damper at the termination to prevent outside air from entering the building when the dryer is not in operation. Screens are not permitted because they would quickly fill with lint and create a blockage.

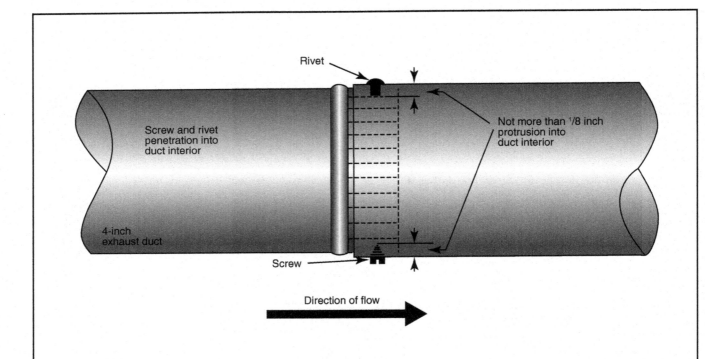

Section 601.9.2 limits screw or fastener penetration into the duct to no more than $^1/_8$ inch. Fasteners are effective in securing duct joints, but longer screws increase lint buildup with the potential for creating an obstruction and fire hazard.

Topic: Dryer Exhaust Power Ventilator
Reference: IFGC 614.5
Category: Specific Appliances
Subject: Clothes Dryer Exhaust

Code Text: *Domestic dryer exhaust duct power ventilators shall be listed and labeled to UL 705 for use in dryer exhaust duct systems. The dryer exhaust duct power ventilator shall be installed in accordance with the manufacturer's instructions.*

Discussion and Commentary: Exhaust ducts that exceed the developed length allowed by the code are a potential fire hazard, create maintenance problems, increase drying times and cause the dryer to be inefficient and waste energy. Domestic dryer exhaust duct power ventilators (DEDPVs), also known as dryer booster fans in the marketplace, increase the airflow in the duct system and can be installed to achieve a greater developed duct length than the code would otherwise allow. DEDPVs are listed to UL 705, which contains requirements for the construction, testing and installation of DEDPVs and requires them to be equipped with features such as interlocks, limit controls, monitoring controls and enunciator devices for safe operation.

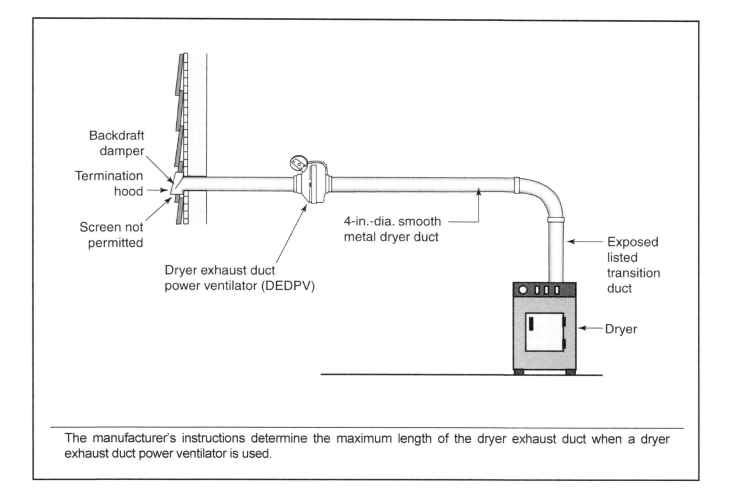

The manufacturer's instructions determine the maximum length of the dryer exhaust duct when a dryer exhaust duct power ventilator is used.

Topic: Makeup Air
Reference: IFGC 614.7

Category: Specific Appliances
Subject: Clothes Dryer Exhaust

Code Text: *Installations exhausting more than 200 cfm (0.09 m³/s) shall be provided with makeup air. Where a closet is designed for the installation of a clothes dryer, an opening having an area of not less than 100 square inches (645 mm²) for makeup air shall be provided in the closet enclosure, or makeup air shall be provided by other approved means.*

Discussion and Commentary: Makeup air is simply air that is provided to replace the air being exhausted. Most residential dryers operate at less than 200 cfm, but in the case of an installation exhausting more than 200 cfm, provisions must be made to bring makeup air to the room. The other requirement for providing makeup air to a dryer occurs when the dryer is intended to be installed in a closet. In this case, the code prescribes an opening with an area not less than 100 square inches to communicate with other spaces.

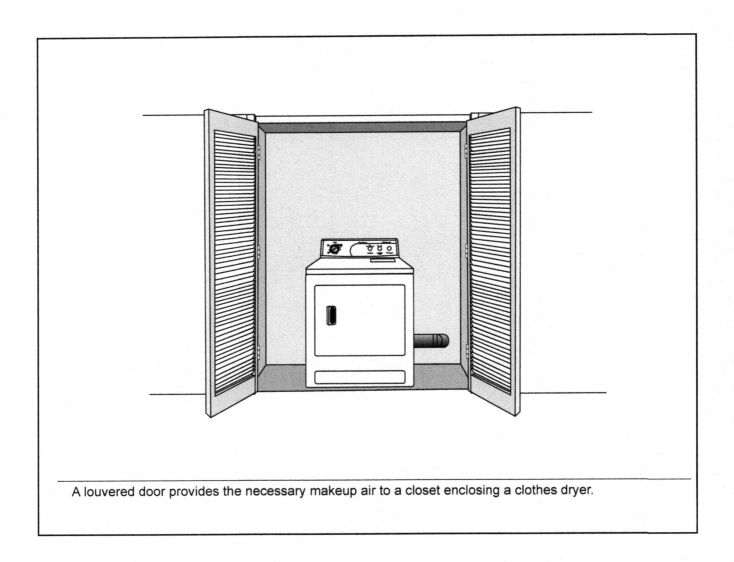

A louvered door provides the necessary makeup air to a closet enclosing a clothes dryer.

Topic: Material and Size
Reference: IFGC 614.9.1
Category: Specific Appliances
Subject: Venting of Appliances

Code Text: *Exhaust ducts shall have a smooth interior finish and shall be constructed of metal a minimum 0.016 inch (0.4 mm) thick. The exhaust duct size shall be 4 inches (102 mm) nominal in diameter.*

Discussion and Commentary: A smooth interior finish helps prevent lint buildup inside the exhaust duct. The code prescribes a nominal 4-inch duct size for optimum performance of a residential dryer exhaust duct. This is not a minimum or maximum number—only 4-inch duct is permitted. For example, increasing the size of duct to 5 inches in diameter would decrease the velocity of the exhaust air and would not be as effective in moving moisture, lint and combustion products to the outdoors.

Residential dryer exhaust duct must be constructed of smooth metal having a minimum thickness of 0.016 inch. This is equivalent to No. 26 gage galvanized steel. A corrugated duct would create friction, decrease flow and trap lint in the duct system and is not permitted by the code.

Topic: Transition Ducts
Reference: IFGC 614.9.3
Category: Specific Appliances
Subject: Clothes Dryer Exhaust

Code Text: *Transition ducts used to connect the dryer to the exhaust duct system shall be a single length that is listed and labeled in accordance with UL 2158A. Transition ducts shall be a maximum of 8 feet (2438 mm) in length, and shall not be concealed within construction.*

Discussion and Commentary: A transition duct is a single length of duct used to connect the dryer discharge outlet to the dryer exhaust system. Although the same restrictions on construction of exhaust duct do not apply to the transition duct (it may be flexible, for example, and not necessarily have a smooth interior surface), in other ways the provisions for transition duct are more restrictive. Transition duct must be listed and labeled, cannot exceed 8 feet in length, and cannot be concealed—all limitations that do not apply to exhaust duct. These tradeoffs intend to allow some flexibility in the transition from the dryer outlet to the exhaust system.

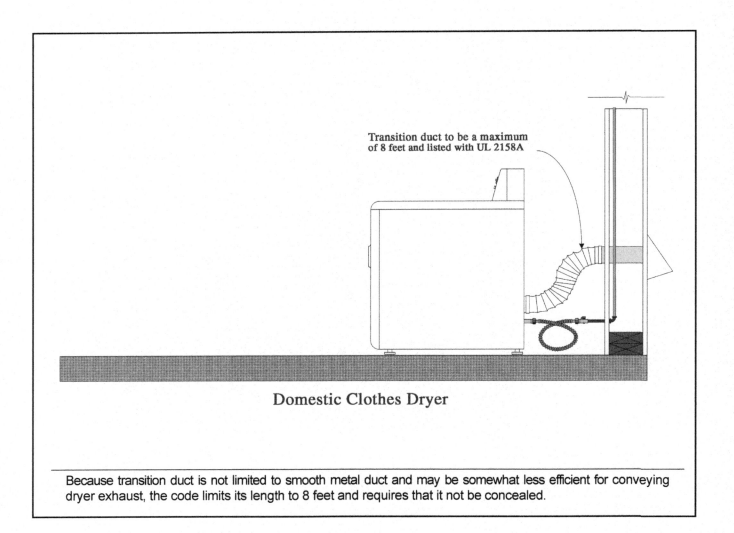

Domestic Clothes Dryer

Because transition duct is not limited to smooth metal duct and may be somewhat less efficient for conveying dryer exhaust, the code limits its length to 8 feet and requires that it not be concealed.

Topic: Duct Length
Reference: IFGC 614.9.4
Category: Specific Appliances
Subject: Clothes Dryer Exhaust

Code Text: *The maximum allowable exhaust duct length shall be determined by one of the methods specified in Sections 614.9.1 through 614.9.4.3.*

Discussion and Commentary: The code provides a choice for determining the maximum length of dryer exhaust duct—the code specified length or a length based on the manufacturer's installation instructions. The maximum specified length in Section 614.9.4.1 is 35 feet. This length is reduced for each fitting based on the fitting radius and the degree of turn in accordance with Table 614.9.4.1. A greater radius (long sweep) duct fitting is more efficient in air flow and therefore represents a smaller equivalent length of duct when compared to a fitting with a smaller radius and tighter turn. The total length is measured from the end of the transition duct to the outside air termination point. The length of the transition duct is not included in this measurement. The code also provides an option to follow the manufacturer's installation instructions, which may permit an exhaust duct length considerably longer than 35 feet.

[M] TABLE 614.9.4.1
DRYER EXHAUST DUCT FITTING EQUIVALENT LENGTH

DRYER EXHAUST DUCT FITTING TYPE	EQUIVALENT LENGTH
4-inch radius mitered 45-degree elbow	2 feet, 6 inches
4-inch radius mitered 90-degree elbow	5 feet
6-inch radius smooth 45-degree elbow	1 foot
6-inch radius smooth 90-degree elbow	1 foot, 9 inches
8-inch radius smooth 45-degree elbow	1 foot
8-inch radius smooth 90-degree elbow	1 foot, 7 inches
10-inch radius smooth 45-degree elbow	9 inches
10-inch radius smooth 90-degree elbow	1 foot, 6 inches

For SI: 1 inch = 25.4 mm, 1 foot = 304.8 mm, 1 degree = 0.01745 rad.

When using the manufacturer's installation instructions for determining the maximum length of dryer exhaust duct, a copy of the installation instructions, including the make and model of the dryer, shall be provided to the code official for verification.

Study Session 8

Topic: Commercial Clothes Dryer
Reference: IFGC 614.10
Category: Specific Appliances
Subject: Clothes Dryer Exhaust

Code Text: *The installation of dryer exhaust ducts serving Type 2 clothes dryers shall comply with the appliance manufacturer's installation instructions. Exhaust fan motors installed in exhaust systems shall be located outside of the airstream. In multiple installations, the fan shall operate continuously or be interlocked to operate when any individual unit is operating. Ducts shall have a minimum clearance of 6 inches (152 mm) to combustible materials.*

Discussion and Commentary: Type 2 clothes dryers are designed for business use and not for typical individual family use. Unlike the prescriptive provisions for domestic clothes dryer exhaust ducts in Section 614.9, commercial dryer exhaust installations primarily rely on the manufacturer's installation instructions. These commercial units move large volumes of air and require makeup air systems to replenish the air exhausted though the ducts to the outside. The material, construction, size and installation of the exhaust ducts also are dependent on the installation instructions based on the specific model of the dryer.

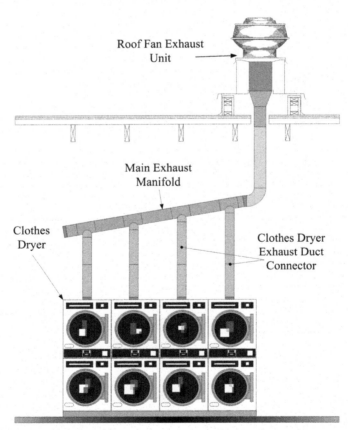

Typical Commercial Clothes Dryer Installation

Because of the high discharge temperature, single-wall exhaust ducts for commercial dryers require a minimum clearance of 6 inches between the ducts and combustibles.

Topic: Common Exhaust in Multistory Structures **Category:** Specific Appliances
Reference: IFGC 614.11 **Subject:** Clothes Dryer Exhaust

Code Text: *Where a common multistory duct system is designed and installed to convey exhaust from multiple clothes dryers, the construction of such system shall be in accordance with all of the following:* The list includes provisions for (1) Shaft construction as required by the IBC, (2) Dampers prohibited and shaft penetrations in accordance with the IMC, (3) Rigid metal ductwork within the shaft to convey the exhaust, (4) Shaft ductwork installed without offsets, (5) Exhaust fan motor in accordance with the IMC, (6) Exhaust fan motor located outside of the airstream, (7) Continuously operating exhaust fan connected to a standby power source, (8) Exhaust fan operation monitored in an approved location, (9) Makeup air provided for the exhaust system, (10) A cleanout opening located at the base of the shaft, (11) Screens not permitted at the termination.

Discussion and Commentary: Dryer exhaust system installation serving multiple dryers in a multistory building requires a rated shaft in accordance with the *International Building Code* (IBC). The IFGC requires No. 26 gage rigid metal ductwork in the shaft to convey the dryer exhaust. Fire and smoke dampers are not permitted in dryer exhaust systems, and the provisions of the *International Mechanical Code* (IMC) compensate for their omission by mandating additional safeguards, including subducts at the shaft penetrations and a continuously operating fan at the upper termination of the exhaust shaft. The importance of the continuously operating fan is emphasized by the requirement for monitoring of the fan operation and the installation of a visual or audible alarm to indicate when the fan is not operating.

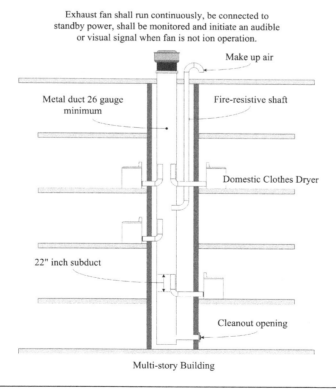

The long list of conditions regulating multiple dryer exhaust shafts in multistory buildings reflects the importance of providing a safe and effective system that conveys moisture, fibers and combustion products to the outside air while maintaining the fire resistance of the shaft and protecting the structural integrity of the building.

Quiz

Study Session 8
IFGC Sections 601 through 614

1. A vented wall furnace shall be located so that a door cannot swing within _____ inches of the air inlet or outlet.

    a. 6
    b. 9
    c. 12
    d. 18

    Reference _____

2. Casing extension boots shall not be installed on a wall furnace unless _____.

    a. constructed of minimum No. 30 gage metal
    b. listed as part of the appliance
    c. included in the manufacturer's installation instructions
    d. supplied by the appliance manufacturer

    Reference _____

3. The floor register of a floor furnace is permitted to be installed _____.

    a. in a stairway landing
    b. 4 inches from a wall.
    c. in a private doorway
    d. 12 inches from draperies

    Reference _____

4. The register of a floor furnace with a horizontal warm air outlet shall not be placed closer than _____ inches to the nearest corner.

   a. 2
   b. 6
   c. 12
   d. 18

   Reference _____

5. Two adjoining sides of the register of a floor furnace shall have a distance of at least _____ inches from walls to provide a walking path.

   a. 24
   b. 18
   c. 36
   d. 12

   Reference _____

6. Floor furnaces shall not be installed _____.

   a. in a concrete floor built on grade
   b. in a wood floor with a crawl space
   c. above a basement
   d. with less than 18 inches clearance above grade

   Reference _____

7. A minimum clearance above grade of _____ inches is required for floor furnaces.

   a. 6
   b. 3
   c. 12
   d. 18

   Reference _____

8. A floor furnace shall have a minimum clearance of 12 inches on all sides except the control side, which shall have a minimum clearance of _____ inches.

   a. 18
   b. 24
   c. 30
   d. 36

   Reference _____

9. Outside ventilation air shall be supplied to the space containing a recirculating direct-fired industrial heater at a minimum rate of _____ cfm per 1,000 Btu/h of the rated input of the heater.

    a. 2   b. 4

    c. 8   d. 16

    Reference _____

10. Clothes dryer exhaust ducts shall be equipped with a _____.

    a. vent connector   b. fire damper

    c. screen   d. backdraft damper

    Reference _____

11. Where susceptible to damage from nails or screws, clothes dryer exhaust ducts shall be protected with shield plates when the duct is installed less than _____ inches from the face of the framing member.

    a. 2   b. $1^3/_4$

    c. $1^1/_2$ d. $1^1/_4$

    Reference _____

12. Screws or other fasteners used to secure joints in clothes dryer exhaust ducts are limited to a maximum of _____-inch penetration into the duct.

    a. $1/_{16}$ b. $3/_{16}$

    c. $1/_8$ d. $1/_4$

    Reference _____

13. Clothes dryer exhaust ducts shall not extend through _____.

    a. attics   b. crawl spaces

    c. plenums   d. concealed spaces

    Reference _____

14. Clothes dryer installations exhausting more than _____ cfm shall be provided with makeup air.

    a. 200   b. 400
    c. 500   d. 600

    Reference _____

15. Where a closet is designed for the installation of a clothes dryer, an opening having an area of not less than _____ square inches shall be provided for makeup air.

    a. 150   b. 50
    c. 200   d. 100

    Reference _____

16. Exhaust ducts for domestic clothes dryers shall have a nominal size of _____ inches in diameter.

    a. 6   b. 5
    c. 4   d. 3

    Reference _____

17. Exhaust ducts for domestic clothes dryers shall be supported at intervals not greater than _____ feet and secured in place.

    a. 3   b. 4
    c. 5   d. 6

    Reference _____

18. When protecting concealed dryer exhaust ducts from penetration by nails or screws, steel shield plates shall have a minimum thickness of _____.

    a. 0.019 inch (26 gage)
    b. 0.024 inch (24 gage)
    c. 0.062 inch (16 gage)
    d. 0.058 inch (14 gage)

    Reference _____

19. For the protection of concealed dryer exhaust ducts, protective shield plates shall extend a minimum of _____ inches above the sole plate and below the top plate.

    a. 2   b. 4
    c. 6   d. 3

    Reference_____

20. Where the dryer exhaust duct equivalent length exceeds _____ feet, a permanent label identifying the length of the duct is required.

    a. 25   b. 45
    c. 35   d. 60

    Reference_____

21. The maximum permitted length of a dryer exhaust duct equipped with a domestic dryer exhaust duct power ventilator is _____.

    a. 35 feet
    b. determined by the dryer manufacturer's instructions
    c. determined by the power ventilator manufacturer's instructions
    d. 50 feet

    Reference_____

22. Installation of a 4-inch-radius mitered 90-degree elbow in a domestic dryer exhaust duct reduces the maximum specified length by _____.

    a. 5 feet   b. 2 feet 6 inches
    c. 1 foot   d. 1 foot 9 inches

    Reference_____

23. Commercial clothes dryer exhaust ducts shall have a minimum clearance of _____ inches to combustible construction.

    a. 2   b. 4
    c. 6   d. 12

    Reference_____

24. The minimum finish dimension for a cleanout opening for a common dryer exhaust system in a multistory building is _____ inches.

    a. 24
    b. 20
    c. 16
    d. 12

Reference_____

25. In a 5-story building, the exhaust shaft serving clothes dryers on each floor requires _____.

    a. a lining of sheet metal or gypsum board
    b. fire dampers in the exhaust duct at each story
    c. a continuously operating exhaust fan
    d. a cleanout opening at each story

Reference_____

Study Session 9

2021 IFGC Sections 615 through 635
Specific Appliances II

OBJECTIVE: To develop an understanding of the provisions for appliances and the regulations governing their installation.

REFERENCE: Sections 615 through 635, 2021 *International Fuel Gas Code*

KEY POINTS:
- What restrictions apply to dampers related to the air inlet of a furnace?
- What separation is required between an outside or return air inlet and a plumbing vent opening?
- What is the minimum volume of a room or space that is the source of return air?
- What restrictions apply to obtaining return air from a room or space where a direct vent appliance is located?
- What are the restrictions when return air is taken from a room or space that contains a solid fueled appliance?
- What locations are prohibited as sources of return air?
- What are the requirements for screen openings that cover an outdoor air inlet?
- When can return air from one dwelling unit be discharged into another dwelling unit?
- What are the requirements for the support of a unit heater?
- What are the required clearances from unit heaters to combustible material?
- What appliances are not permitted to be used a primary source of heat in a dwelling unit?
- What are the restrictions on the input ratings of unvented room heaters?
- What is the maximum Btu/h per cubic foot of room volume for an unvented room heater?
- What type of mandatory safety device shall be installed on an unvented room heater?
- The installation of commercial cooking appliances is not permitted in what occupancies?

KEY POINTS:
(Cont'd)

- What are the listing and labeling requirements for household type cooking appliances installed in dwelling units?
- What methods are permitted for reducing the required clearances between a household cooking appliance and combustible material?
- What are the requirements for installing a microwave oven over a listed cooking appliance?
- What conditions are placed on the installation of gas piping serving cooling and heating appliances?
- What governs the clearances between a gas-fired air conditioning unit and combustible material?
- What are the requirements for installing a gas-fired air conditioner on a combustible surface?
- What are the support requirements for illuminating appliances that are attached to walls or ceilings?

Topic: Heat and Time Controls
Reference: IFGC 615.6
Category: Specific Appliances
Subject: Sauna Heaters

Code Text: *Sauna heaters shall be equipped with a thermostat which will limit room temperature to 194°F (90°C). If the thermostat is not an integral part of the sauna heater, the heat-sensing element shall be located within 6 inches (152 mm) of the ceiling. If the heat-sensing element is a capillary tube and bulb, the assembly shall be attached to the wall or other support, and shall be protected against physical damage.*

Discussion and Commentary: Limiting the room temperature of a sauna room is an important safeguard to reduce the risk of a heat-related injury. To protect users from excessive heat while in a sauna, the heat-sensing element of the thermostat must be located within 6 inches of the ceiling, ensuring that it measures the highest temperatures in the room. Heat-sensing elements subject to physical damage must be protected and securely anchored to the wall.

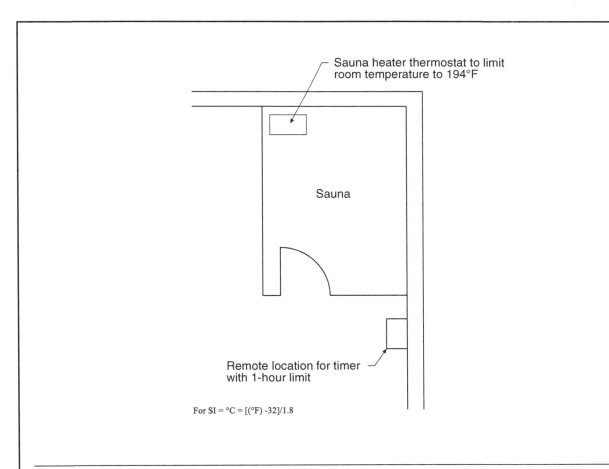

Timers are not required by the code but are an additional safety measure to protect the occupants from prolonged exposure to heat and to protect the building from fire hazards. When installed, the timer must be located on the exterior of the sauna room, requiring the user to leave the sauna to reset the timer, thereby reducing the chances of overexposure.

Topic: Sauna Room Ventilation
Reference: IFGC 615.7
Category: Specific Applications
Subject: Sauna Heaters

Code Text: *A ventilation opening into the sauna room shall be provided. The opening shall be not less than 4 inches by 8 inches (102 mm by 203 mm) located near the top of the door into the sauna room.*

Discussion and Commentary: A ventilation opening provides a means for excess heat and steam to exit the sauna room while providing ventilation air for the occupants.

Minimum size of 4 inches by 8 inches opening located near the top of the door

Sauna Room Door

Because heat and steam rise, the ventilation opening is required to be located near the top of the door.

Topic: Warning Notice
Reference: IFGC 615.7.1
Category: Specific Appliances
Subject: Sauna Heaters

Code Text: *The following permanent notice, constructed of approved material, shall be mechanically attached to the sauna room on the outside: WARNING: DO NOT EXCEED 30 MINUTES IN SAUNA. EXCESSIVE EXPOSURE CAN BE HARMFUL TO HEALTH. ANY PERSON WITH POOR HEALTH SHOULD CONSULT A PHYSICIAN BEFORE USING SAUNA. The words shall contrast with the background and the wording shall be in letters not less than $1/4$ inch (6.4 mm) high.* See the exception for one- and two-family dwellings.

Discussion and Commentary: A warning must be posted to alert users of the potential hazard associated with prolonged exposure to high temperature and humidity levels. Because the sign is mechanically attached to the outside of the sauna room, users will be more aware of the potential hazards.

WARNING: DO NOT EXCEED 30 MINUTES IN SAUNA. EXCESSIVE EXPOSURE CAN BE HARMFUL TO HEALTH. ANY PERSON WITH POOR HEALTH SHOULD CONSULT A PHYSICIAN BEFORE USING SAUNA.

A sauna warning sign is not required in one- and two-family dwellings, where users are more familiar with their surroundings.

Study Session 9

Topic: Prohibited Sources
Reference: IFGC 618.3
Category: Specific Appliances
Subject: Forced-Air Warm-Air Furnaces

Code Text: *Outside or return air for forced-air heating and cooling systems shall not be taken from the following locations:* The list includes: (1) Inlets closer than 10 feet from an appliance vent outlet, plumbing vent opening or exhaust fan discharge outlet, unless the outlet is 3 feet above the outside air inlet; (2) Where there is the presence of objectionable odors, fumes or flammable vapors; or where located less than 10 feet above the surface of any abutting public way or driveway; or where located at grade level by a sidewalk, street, alley or driveway; (3) A hazardous or insanitary location or refrigeration machinery room, (4) A room or space with inadequate volume, (5) A room or space containing an appliance where such a room or space serves as the sole source of return air (see the exceptions), (6) A closet, bathroom, toilet room, kitchen, garage, mechanical room, boiler room, furnace room or attic (see the exception); (7) A crawl space by means of direct connection to the return side of a forced-air system. Transfer openings are permitted.

Discussion and Commentary: Return air typically is taken from the spaces or areas being conditioned, but there are locations in a building that may contaminate the circulating air or have an insufficient volume of air and are not permitted as suitable sources of return air. Similarly, outdoor air must be obtained from locations that are free of such contaminants as flue gases, sewer gas, vehicle exhaust or hazardous vapors. The prescribed clearances to outside contaminate sources intend to ensure that a fresh air supply is circulated throughout the building.

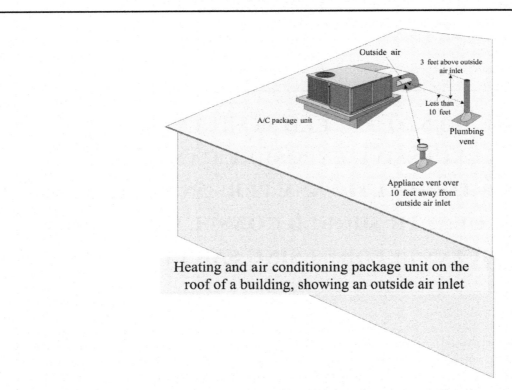

Heating and air conditioning package unit on the roof of a building, showing an outside air inlet

---

It is not the intent to prohibit return air from being obtained from any room containing less than 25 percent of the total volume of the entire conditioned area. Small rooms, such as bedrooms, are permitted as sources of return air, provided the amount of return air does not exceed the amount of supply air discharging to that room.

Topic: Support
Reference: IFGC 620.2
Category: Specific Appliances
Subject: Unit Heaters

Code Text: *Suspended-type unit heaters shall be supported by elements that are designed and constructed to accommodate the weight and dynamic loads. Hangers and brackets shall be of noncombustible material.*

Discussion and Commentary: Brackets, pipes, rods, angle iron and fasteners used in the suspension of unit heaters are required to be noncombustible materials. The supporting structure and the mounting supports shall be designed for the dead loads and the dynamic loads. Of primary concern is a support failure and the potential for fire, explosion or injury to the building or its occupants.

Unit heaters are warm air space heaters that are self-contained and commonly located in garages, workshops, warehouses, factories, mercantile and similar large open buildings. They are typically not designed to move air through ductwork.

Topic: Clearances
Reference: IFGC 620.4
Category: Specific Appliances
Subject: Unit Heaters

Code Text: Suspended-type unit heaters shall be installed with clearances to combustible materials of not less than 18 inches (457 mm) at the sides, 12 inches (305 mm) at the bottom and 6 inches (152 mm) above the top where the unit heater has an internal draft hood or 1 inch (25 mm) above the top of the sloping side of the vertical draft hood. Floor-mounted-type unit heaters shall be installed with clearances to combustible materials at the back and one side only of not less than 6 inches (152 mm). Where the flue gases are vented horizontally, the 6-inch (152 mm) clearance shall be measured from the draft hood or vent instead of the rear wall of the unit heater. Floor-mounted-type unit heaters shall not be installed on combustible floors unless listed for such installation. Clearances for servicing all unit heaters shall be in accordance with the manufacturer's installation instructions. See the exception for reduced clearances provided by the manufacturer.

Discussion and Commentary: Of primary concern in the installation of unit heaters is to provide adequate clearances to prevent ignition of nearby combustible materials and to provide ventilation for proper operation of the equipment. The code addresses these concerns by providing minimum clearance dimensions for both suspended and floor-mounted heaters.

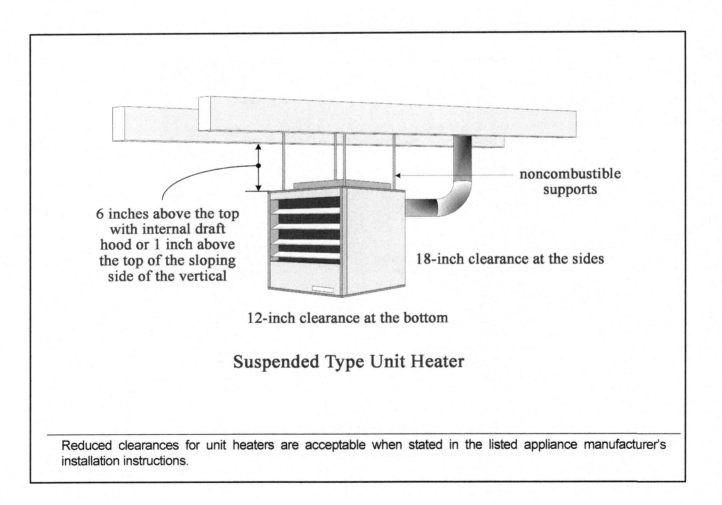

Reduced clearances for unit heaters are acceptable when stated in the listed appliance manufacturer's installation instructions.

Topic: Prohibited Use
Reference: IFGC 621.2
Category: Specific Appliances
Subject: Unvented Room Heaters

Code Text: *One or more unvented room heaters shall not be used as the sole source of comfort heating in a dwelling unit.*

Discussion and Commentary: Although they may supplement other sources of heating, unvented room heaters are limited in heat output and are regarded as secondary heaters and not intended to replace approved listed appliances as the primary source of heat. One or more unvented room heaters used as the primary source of heat would not distribute heat effectively and likely would need to run continuously, which is not anticipated in their design.

The code requires unvented room heaters to be tested in accordance with ANSI Z21.11.2 and installed in accordance with the listing and the manufacturer's installation instructions.

Topic: Room or Space Volume
Reference: IFGC 621.5
Category: Specific Appliances
Subject: Unvented Room Heaters

Code Text: *The aggregate input rating of all unvented appliances installed in a room or space shall not exceed 20 Btu/h per cubic foot (207 W/m³) of volume of such room or space. Where the room or space in which the appliances are installed is directly connected to another room or space by a doorway, archway or other opening of comparable size that cannot be closed, the volume of such adjacent room or space shall be permitted to be included in the calculations.*

Discussion and Commentary: Unvented room heaters require combustion air the same as vented room heaters. Unlike vented appliances that vent their products of combustion through venting systems to the outdoors, unvented room heaters vent their products of combustion into the room or space inside the building. The prescribed volume of air is necessary to sufficiently dilute these combustion products and maintain a healthy living environment.

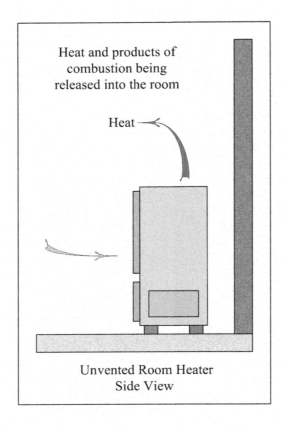

Unvented Room Heater
Side View

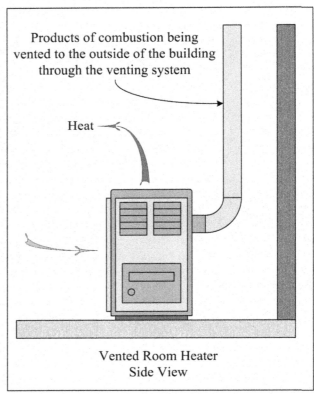

Vented Room Heater
Side View

Adjoining rooms may be included as contributing to the required volume of air provided they are connected with a permanent doorway without a door.

Topic: Oxygen-Depletion Safety System **Category:** Specific Appliances
Reference: IFGC 621.6 **Subject:** Unvented Room Heaters

Code Text: *Unvented room heaters shall be equipped with an oxygen-depletion-sensitive safety shut-off system. The system shall shut off the gas supply to the main and pilot burners when the oxygen in the surrounding atmosphere is depleted to the percent concentration specified by the manufacturer, but not lower than 18 percent. The system shall not incorporate field adjustment means capable of changing the set point at which the system acts to shut off the gas supply to the room heater.*

Discussion and Commentary: To protect occupants from the ill health effects of increased concentrations of combustion products, an oxygen depletion switch is required on unvented room heaters. These devices sense the oxygen content in the room and shut down the fuel supply to the heater when the device senses oxygen levels below the predetermined level. Adequate levels of oxygen in the combustion air are required for proper operation of the appliance and to prevent the formation of carbon monoxide caused by incomplete combustion.

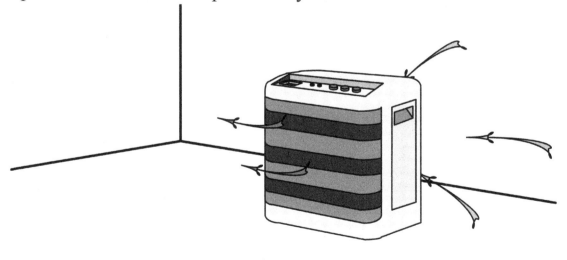

Oxygen-depletion safety systems typically have a latching device, meaning that after the unit shuts down owing to activation of the oxygen sensor, the unvented heater does not reset and turn back on automatically. Instead, the heater typically requires a manual reset device.

Topic: Prohibited Location
Reference: IFGC 623.2

Category: Specific Appliances
Subject: Cooking Appliances

Code Text: *Cooking appliances designed, tested, listed and labeled for use in commercial occupancies shall not be installed within dwelling units or within any area where domestic cooking operations occur.*

Exception: Appliances that are also listed as domestic cooking appliances.

Discussion and Commentary: Commercial cooking appliances are tested to different standards than residential cooking appliances. Some of the safety features that are typical on residential appliances, such as insulation for protection against burns, are not installed on commercial types of appliances. Commercial cooking equipment operates at higher temperatures, requires greater clearances, has less insulation and requires increased ventilation when compared to domestic cooking appliances. The exception recognizes that gas cooking appliances may be tested and listed to both commercial and domestic standards and may be installed in dwelling units.

Domestic cooking appliances require a greater degree of user protection than commercial cooking appliances. The code generally does not permit commercial cooking appliances to be installed in a dwelling unit or in any location where domestic-type cooking operations occur.

Topic: Vertical Clearance above Cooking Top **Category:** Specific Appliances
Reference: IFGC 623.7 **Subject:** Cooking Appliances

Code Text: *Household cooking appliances shall have a vertical clearance above the cooking top of not less than 30 inches (760 mm) to combustible material and metal cabinets. A minimum clearance of 24 inches (610 mm) is permitted where one of the following is installed:* The list of alternatives includes: (1) The underside of the combustible material or metal cabinet above the cooking top is protected with not less than $^{1}/_{4}$-inch (6 mm) insulating millboard covered with sheet metal not less than 0.0122 inch (0.3 mm) thick, (2) A metal ventilating hood constructed of sheet metal not less than 0.0122 inch (0.3 mm) thick is installed above the cooking top with a clearance of not less than $^{1}/_{4}$ inch (6.4 mm) between the hood and the underside of the combustible material or metal cabinet. The hood shall have a width not less than the width of the appliance and shall be centered over the appliance, (3) A listed cooking appliance or microwave oven is installed over a listed cooking appliance and in compliance with the terms of the manufacturer's installation instructions for the upper appliance.

Discussion and Commentary: In general, the minimum clearance between a domestic cook top and the underneath side of combustible or metal cabinets shall not be less than 30 inches. However, clearances may be reduced to 24 inches, provided the underside of the cabinet is protected in some manner to reduce the possibility of cabinets or their contents igniting or overheating.

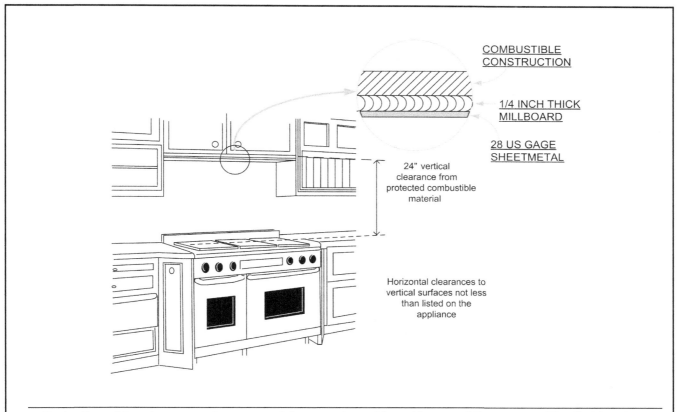

Reduction of the clearance above a cook top may be achieved in one of three ways. The first involves the installation of insulating millboard covered with sheet metal. However, protection is more commonly provided with a range hood with an air space above it, or with the installation of a listed microwave that is approved for the location.

Topic: Plenums and Air Ducts
Reference: IFGC 627.7
Category: Specific Appliances
Subject: Air Conditioning Appliances

Code Text: *A plenum supplied as a part of the air-conditioning appliance shall be installed in accordance with the appliance manufacturer's instructions. Where a plenum is not supplied with the appliance, such plenum shall be installed in accordance with the fabrication and installation instructions provided by the plenum and appliance manufacturer. The method of connecting supply and return ducts shall facilitate proper circulation of air. Where the air-conditioning appliance is installed within a space separated from the spaces served by the appliance, the air circulated by the appliance shall be conveyed by ducts that are sealed to the casing of the appliance and that separate the circulating air from the combustion and ventilation air.*

Discussion and Commentary: As part of the air conditioning duct system, plenums are used to distribute conditioned air (or return air) into ducts run to various locations in the conditioned space. Plenums must be installed in accordance with the appliance manufacturer's installation instructions. Requirements also include the sealing of ductwork in the air conditioning system to isolate the circulating air from combustion and ventilation air.

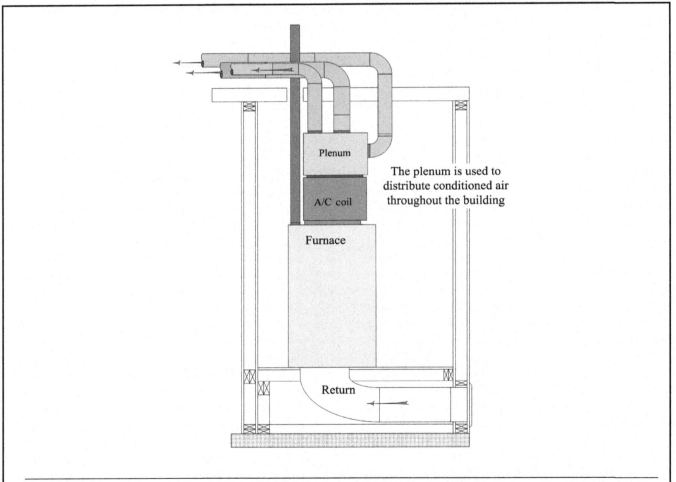

Additional requirements for sheet metal plenums are found in Chapter 6 of the *International Mechanical Code* (IMC).

Study Session 9
IFGC Sections 615 through 635

1. Sauna heaters shall be equipped with a thermostat that limits the room temperature to no more than _____ degrees Fahrenheit.

    a. 175
    b. 194
    c. 200
    d. 210

    Reference _____

2. The required ventilation opening to a sauna room shall be not less than _____ inches by _____ inches.

    a. 4, 8
    b. 8, 8
    c. 4, 12
    d. 8, 12

    Reference _____

3. In general, return air for a forced air furnace shall not be taken from a _____.

    a. room containing a direct vent appliance
    b. crawl space
    c. room containing an unvented appliance
    d. room containing a solid fuel appliance

    Reference _____

4. The minimum unobstructed total area of the outside and return air ducts or openings to a forced-air warm-air furnace shall be not less than _____ square inch(es) per 1,000 Btu/h output rating capacity of the furnace.

   a. 6
   b. 4
   c. 3
   d. 2

   Reference _____

5. The minimum unobstructed total area of supply ducts from a forced-air warm-air furnace shall be not less than _____ square inch(es) per 1,000 Btu/h output rating capacity of the furnace.

   a. 1
   b. 4
   c. 2
   d. 6

   Reference _____

6. Unless the prescribed vertical clearance dimensions are maintained, the inlet for outside or return air for a forced-air heating system shall not be located less than _____ feet horizontally from a plumbing vent termination.

   a. 8
   b. 12
   c. 5
   d. 10

   Reference _____

7. Required outdoor air inlets for a residential forced-air heating system shall be covered with screen having _____-inch openings.

   a. 1
   b. $3/4$
   c. $1/2$
   d. $1/4$

   Reference _____

8. In general, return air for a forced-air heating system is permitted to be obtained from a(n) _____.

   a. garage
   b. attic
   c. sleeping room
   d. kitchen

   Reference _____

9. Hangers for a suspended unit heater must be _____.
   a. designed by a registered design professional
   b. steel angle iron
   c. provided by the appliance manufacturer
   d. noncombustible

   Reference _____

10. Suspended type unit heaters shall be installed with clearances to combustible materials of not less than _____ inches at the sides of the unit.
    a. 6   b. 12
    c. 18   d. 24

    Reference _____

11. The input rating of unvented room heaters is limited to a maximum _____ Btu/h.
    a. 14,000   b. 28,000
    c. 40,000   d. 54,000

    Reference _____

12. Unvented room heaters shall not be installed within Group _____ occupancies.
    a. E   b. B
    c. F   d. M

    Reference _____

13. Unless a higher limit is set by the manufacturer of an unvented room heater, a required oxygen-depletion safety system shall shut off the appliance when the oxygen is depleted to _____ percent concentration.
    a. 18   b. 8
    c. 38   d. 28

    Reference _____

14. Cooking appliances installed in areas where domestic cooking operations occur shall be listed and labeled as _____-type appliances for domestic use.

    a. residential   b. noncommercial
    c. household   d. dwelling

    Reference _____

15. A domestic open top broiler shall have a minimum clearance of _____ inches between the cooking top and combustible material above the hood.

    a. 30   b. 36
    c. 18   d. 24

    Reference _____

16. Unless provisions are made for a reduced clearance, domestic cooking appliances shall have a vertical clearance above the cooking top of not less than _____ inches to combustible material and metal cabinets above.

    a. 18   b. 24
    c. 30   d. 42

    Reference _____

17. Where the underside of the combustible material or metal cabinet above a cooking top is protected with $^1/_4$-inch insulating millboard covered with sheet metal, a vertical clearance of not less than _____ inches is permitted above a domestic cooking appliance.

    a. 18   b. 24
    c. 30   d. 12

    Reference _____

18. Water heaters utilized both to supply potable water and provide hot water for space-heating shall be listed and labeled and shall be installed in accordance with the _____.

    a. *International Fuel Gas Code* (IFGC)
    b. *International Plumbing Code* (IPC)
    c. *International Mechanical Code* (IMC)
    d. *International Building Code* (IBC)

    Reference _____

19. The required permanent notice placed outside of a sauna room warns users to not exceed _____ minutes in the sauna.

    a. 30   b. 60

    c. 15   d. 45

    Reference_____

20. If a thermostat is not an integral part of the sauna heater, the heat-sensing element shall be located a maximum of _____ inches below the ceiling.

    a. 8   b. 4

    c. 12   d. 6

    Reference_____

21. A means to interrupt the electrical supply to a gas-fired air-conditioning appliance shall be provided within sight of and not more than _____ feet from the appliance.

    a. 25   b. 50

    c. 75   d. 100

    Reference_____

22. The minimum clearance to combustible material from the back of a floor-mounted unit heater is _____ inches.

    a. 18   b. 12

    c. 6   d. 4

    Reference_____

23. A 4-foot high post supporting an illuminating appliance shall be equivalent in strength to a _____-inch diameter Schedule 40 steel pipe.

    a. 3   b. $2\frac{1}{2}$

    c. 1   d. $\frac{3}{4}$

    Reference_____

24. An outdoor air ventilation rate of not less than _____ cfm per 1,000 Btu/h of aggregate input rating is required for unvented infrared heaters.

    a. 4   b. 20

    c. 40   d. 75

    Reference_____

25. When provided, a timer controlling the main burner of a sauna is limited to a maximum operating time of _____ minutes.

    a. 30   b. 60

    c. 90   d. 120

    Reference_____

2021 IFGC Chapter 7
Gaseous Hydrogen Systems

OBJECTIVE: To gain an understanding of the code provisions that apply to gaseous hydrogen systems, including hydrogen generating and refueling operations, ventilation, approved locations, piping installation and piping testing.

REFERENCE: Chapter 7, 2021 *International Fuel Gas Code*

KEY POINTS:
- When is a ventilation system required for a hydrogen-generating appliance?
- Which codes are referenced for ventilation?
- What restrictions apply to valves located in pressure relief piping?
- What provisions apply to the termination of pressure relief devices?
- What are the access requirements for pressure relief valves?
- What markings are required to identify piping for hydrogen systems?
- What materials are acceptable for piping in hydrogen systems?
- When does hydrogen piping require protection from physical damage?
- What are the requirements for joints in piping and tubing in hydrogen systems?
- What code regulates the handling of compressed gas?
- What is the minimum allowable test pressure for a hydrostatic leak test?
- What is the minimum allowable test pressure for a pneumatic leak test?
- How do the test criteria change when the pressure test exceeds 125 psig?
- What is approved media for pressure testing?
- What is the minimum amount of time a system must be under pressure during a leak test?
- What requirements apply to test gauges?
- How does the test pressure affect the maximum pressure gage increments?
- What items must be exposed for examination during a pressure test?
- What are the limits for a drop in pressure during a leak test?

KEY POINTS:
(Cont'd)
- Purged gases must discharge to what location?
- What is the minimum above-ground clearance for the termination of a vent pipe for purging?
- What agency regulates the purging of hydrogen systems?

Topic: Generating and Refueling
Reference: IFGC 703.1
Category: Gaseous Hydrogen Systems
Subject: General Requirements

Code Text: *Hydrogen-generating and refueling appliances shall be installed and located in accordance with their listing and the manufacturer's instructions. Exhaust ventilation shall be required in public garages, private garages, repair garages, automotive motor fuel-dispensing facilities and parking garages that contain hydrogen-generating appliances or refueling systems in accordance with NFPA 2. For the purpose of this section, rooms or spaces that are not part of the living space of a dwelling unit and that communicate directly with a private garage through openings shall be considered to be part of the private garage.*

Discussion and Commentary: To prevent accumulation of flammable hydrogen gas in a space as a result of a leak, the code requires ventilation of the applicable spaces containing hydrogen generating or refueling operations. Ventilation is very effective in limiting the concentration of hydrogen gas in a space, as hydrogen gas is buoyant and disperses readily in the air. Natural or mechanical ventilation is required to remove and prevent the accumulation of hydrogen gas. For natural ventilation, the code prescribes the necessary ventilation opening sizes and locations to prevent a hydrogen gas/air mixture that could exceed 25 percent of the lower flammable limit.

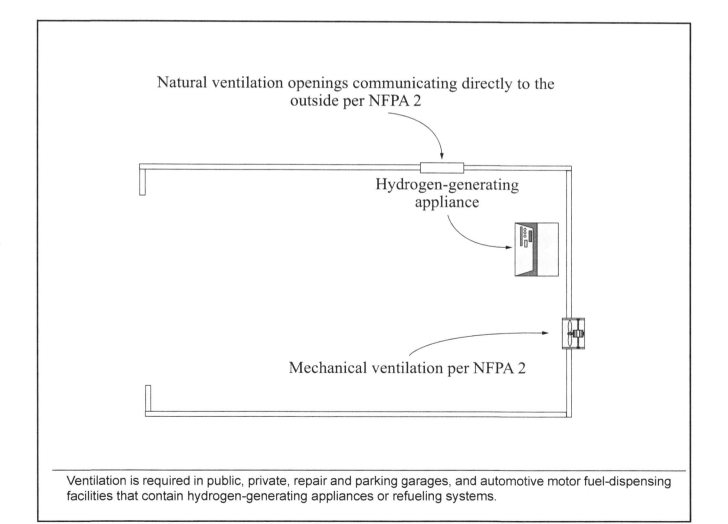

Ventilation is required in public, private, repair and parking garages, and automotive motor fuel-dispensing facilities that contain hydrogen-generating appliances or refueling systems.

Topic: Relief Valves	Category: Gaseous Hydrogen Systems
Reference: IFGC 703.3.2	Subject: General Requirements

Code Text: *Valves and other mechanical restrictions shall not be located between the pressure relief device and the point of release to the atmosphere.*

Discussion and Commentary: A relief valve is a safety device that protects a compressed gas container against the hazard of over-pressurization. Over-pressurization can occur if the cylinder is exposed to excessive heat from a fire. Installing a valve between the relief valve and the point of discharge to the outside air would provide a means to disable the relief valve and render it useless.

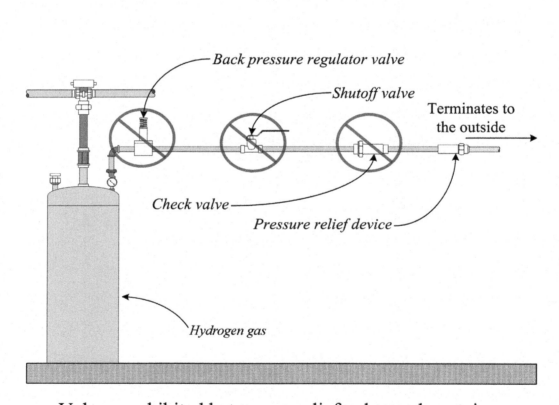

Valves prohibited between a relief valve and container

Because of the high pressures and cold temperatures associated with the storage of hydrogen gas, pressure relief devices are required on all gaseous hydrogen containers. Shutoff valves, check valves or other mechanical restrictions are prohibited on either the upstream or downstream side of the pressure relief device so that there are no obstructions in the vent line other than the relief valve from the container to the termination point.

Topic: Relief Valve Sizing
Reference: IFGC 703.3.5

Category: Gaseous Hydrogen Systems
Subject: General Requirements

Code Text: *Pressure relief devices shall be sized in accordance with the specifications to which the container was fabricated. The relief device shall be sized to prevent the maximum design pressure of the container or system from being exceeded.*

Discussion and Commentary: The code requires the design of the venting system to allow for the discharge of the cylinder contents without exceeding the design pressure of the cylinder or the hydrogen storage and dispensing system.

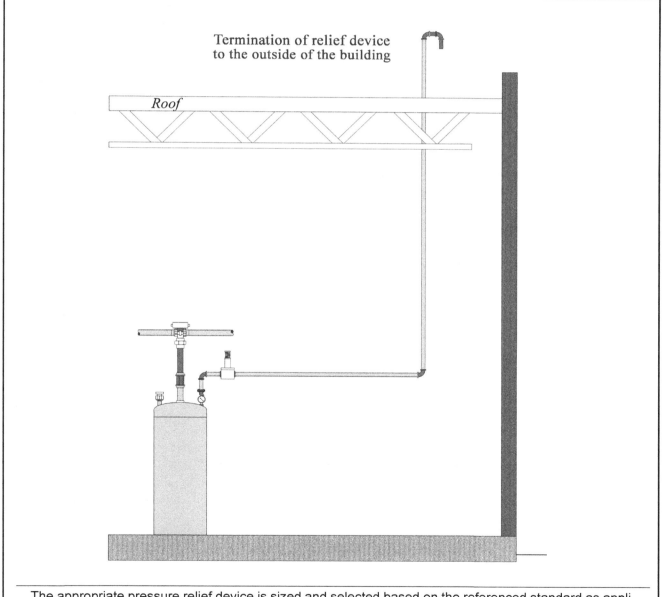

The appropriate pressure relief device is sized and selected based on the referenced standard as applicable to the particular type of storage container.

Study Session 10

Topic: Relief Valve Termination
Reference: IFGC 703.3.8
Category: Gaseous Hydrogen Systems
Subject: General Requirements

Code Text: *Pressure relief devices shall be arranged to discharge unobstructed in accordance with Section 2309 of the* International Fire Code. *Discharge shall be directed to the outdoors in such a manner as to prevent impingement of escaping gas on personnel, containers, equipment and adjacent structures and to prevent introduction of escaping gas into enclosed spaces. The discharge shall not terminate under eaves or canopies.* See the exception for DOTn-specified containers with an internal volume of 2 cubic feet (0.057 m^3) or less.

Discussion and Commentary: With the exception of US DOT-specification cylinders with an internal volume of 2 cubic feet, Section 703.3.8 and the IFC require pressure relief devices for compressed gas hydrogen systems to be terminated outside a building. The vent piping must be arranged in such a way that any pressure release of hydrogen gas discharges to open air, is not trapped under overhangs or in enclosures and does not create additional hazards to personnel, equipment or buildings.

Pressure relief devices shall be arranged and terminated in accordance with Section 2309 of the *International Fire Code* (IFC).

Topic: Identification of Hydrogen Piping Systems **Category:** Gaseous Hydrogen Systems
Reference: IFGC 704.1.2.2 **Subject:** Piping, Use and Handling

Code Text: *Hydrogen piping systems shall be marked in accordance with ANSI A13.1. Markings used for piping systems shall consist of the name of the contents and shall include a direction-of-flow arrow. Markings shall be provided at all of the following locations:*

   1. *At each valve.*
   2. *At wall, floor and ceiling penetrations.*
   3. *At each change of direction.*
   4. *At intervals not exceeding 20 feet (6096 mm).*

Discussion and Commentary: The provisions for labeling gaseous hydrogen piping systems are more stringent than those for labeling LP gas and natural gas piping. Hydrogen piping systems require a label at every change of direction, every valve, each penetration and every 20 feet of piping in accordance with ANSI A13.1. The reason for these requirements is to ensure fire fighters have a means of identifying these systems so that they can rapidly trace the hydrogen flow path from the source supply to the point of use.

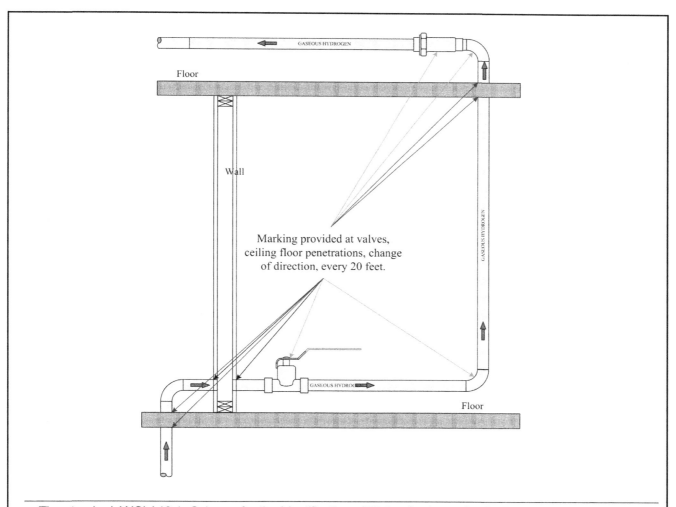

The standard ANSI A13.1, *Scheme for the Identification of Piping Systems*, details the valve and piping color coding, painting and labeling methods used in the United States.

Topic: Prohibited Locations
Reference: IFGC 704.1.2.3.1
Category: Gaseous Hydrogen Systems
Subject: Piping, Use and Handling

Code Text: *Piping shall not be installed in or through a circulating air duct; clothes chute; chimney or gas vent; ventilating duct; dumbwaiter; or elevator shaft. Piping shall not be concealed or covered by the surface of any wall, floor or ceiling.*

Discussion and Commentary: Restrictions on the locations of hydrogen gas piping reflect a cautious approach based on the properties and nature of the gas, which in certain concentrations mixed with oxygen may ignite explosively. In part, these restrictions intend to prevent hydrogen gas from being circulated throughout the building if a leak should develop. Equally important is the concern that piping exposed to the circulating air system and the resulting temperature differentials may cause condensation, corrosion and eventual failure of the piping or its connections.

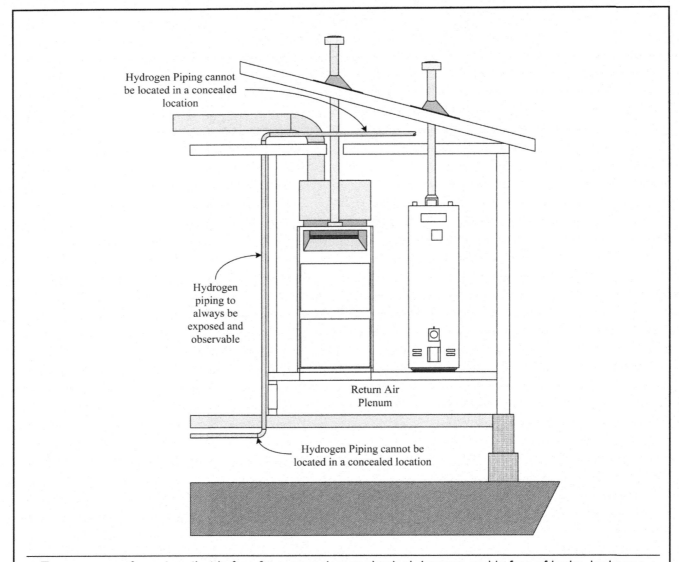

To ensure a safe system that is free from corrosion or physical damage and is free of leaks, hydrogen piping must always be exposed for inspection and maintenance.

Topic: Electrical Continuity
Reference: IFGC 704.1.2.4.2
Category: Gaseous Hydrogen Systems
Subject: Piping, Use and Handling

Code Text: *Mechanical joints shall maintain electrical continuity through the joint or a bonding jumper shall be installed around the joint.*

Discussion and Commentary: Bonding is the permanent joining of metallic parts to form an electrically conductive path to ensure electrical continuity. A bonding jumper connects to the metallic piping in an approved manner at both sides of a nonconducting joint or coupling to maintain the conductive path. In the case of gaseous hydrogen piping, bonding at mechanical joints is required to control and safely dissipate a static electricity accumulation and to prevent the ignition of leaking hydrogen gas.

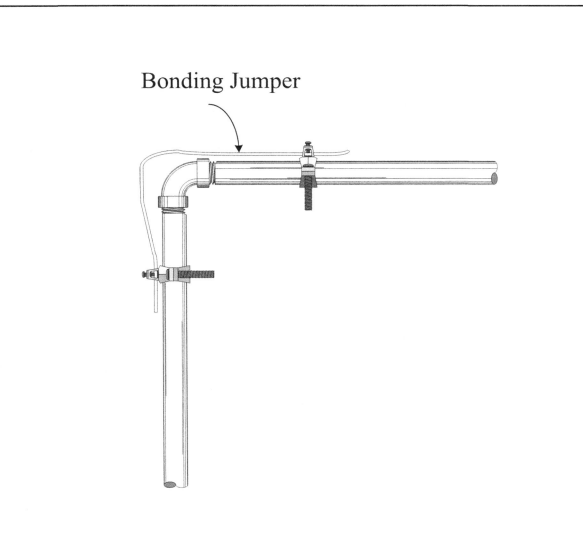

Welded joints provide an electrically conductive path that makes a bonding jumper unnecessary. Mechanical joints are permitted, but if they are not approved for electrical bonding, then a bonding jumper is required to provide electrical continuity throughout the piping system and to provide an added level of safety.

Quiz

Study Session 10
IFGC Chapter 7

1. Hydrogen pressure relief devices require _____.
   a. check valves
   b. protection from freezing
   c. ready access
   d. locked-open valves

   Reference _____

2. Hydrogen-generating and refueling appliances located in automotive motor fuel-dispensing facilities and repair garages _____.
   a. are limited to a storage capacity of 250 cubic feet
   b. require exhaust ventilation
   c. must comply with NFPA 72
   d. shall be enclosed in a separate hydrogen fuel-gas room

   Reference _____

3. The nontoxic gas in a gaseous hydrogen system must contain not less than _____ percent hydrogen by volume.
   a. 90
   b. 95
   c. 98
   d. 99.5

   Reference _____

4. When located in a private garage of a single-family dwelling regulated by the *International Residential Code*, gaseous hydrogen storage cylinders shall not exceed a capacity of _____ cubic feet.
   a. 50
   b. 150
   c. 250
   d. 350

   Reference _____

5. For working pressures at or above 125 psig, the pneumatic test pressure on gaseous hydrogen piping systems shall be not less than _____ percent of the maximum working pressure.

    a. 60   b. 110

    c. 75   d. 120

Reference _____

6. Gaseous hydrogen piping is not allowed _____.

    a. in an exposed location indoors

    b. in underground locations

    c. to penetrate an outer foundation wall underground

    d. less than 16 inches above grade in an outdoor location

Reference _____

7. Compressed gas containers, cylinders and tanks, except those with a water volume less than _____ gallons and those designed for use in a horizontal position, shall be used in an upright position with the valve end up.

    a. 2.3   b. 1.3

    c. 3.3   d. 4.3

Reference _____

8. Hydrogen piping systems shall be provided with markings at intervals not exceeding _____ feet.

    a. 20   b. 25

    c. 8   d. 16

Reference _____

9. Valves including shutoffs, check valves and other mechanical restrictions shall not be installed between a hydrogen storage container and a _____.

    a. hydrogen generating appliance

    b. fuel dispenser

    c. pressure vessel

    d. pressure relief device

Reference _____

10. Piping, tubing and fittings conveying gaseous hydrogen shall be designed and installed in accordance with the IFGC and the _____.

    a. listing agency
    b. *International Mechanical Code* (IMC)
    c. *International Building Code* (IBC)
    d. *International Fire Code* (IFC)

    Reference _____

11. Hydrogen piping systems shall be provided with markings at each _____.

    a. hanger or anchor
    b. connector
    c. appliance
    d. wall penetration

    Reference _____

12. The IFGC requires piping and tubing for hydrogen gas systems to be listed or approved for the application, or the materials must be _____.

    a. cast iron
    b. polyethylene
    c. 300 series stainless steel
    d. CSST

    Reference _____

13. For a hydrogen piping system, the pneumatic test pressure shall be not less than _____ psig.

    a. 5
    b. 10
    c. 25
    d. 50

    Reference _____

14. Brazing alloys used for joints in hydrogen piping systems shall have a melting point greater than _____ degrees Fahrenheit.

    a. 500
    b. 750
    c. 1,000
    d. 1,500

    Reference _____

15. Mechanical joints in a hydrogen piping system that do not maintain electrical continuity through the joint require a _____.
    a. ground conductor
    b. grounding terminal
    c. bonding bushing
    d. bonding jumper

    Reference_____

16. Prior to system operation, a hydrogen piping system shall have an inspection conducted or verified by the _____.
    a. equipment manufacturer
    b. engineer of record
    c. code official
    d. special inspector

    Reference_____

17. The hydrostatic test pressure on a hydrogen piping system shall be not less than _____ psig.
    a. 50
    b. 100
    c. 150
    d. 200

    Reference _____

18. Which method of pipe assembly is limited to installations within hydrogen cutoff rooms or installations outside of buildings?
    a. flange connections
    b. welded connection
    c. brazed connections
    d. compression fittings

    Reference_____

19. The minimum test duration on a hydrogen piping system shall be _____ minutes.
    a. 15
    b. 30
    c. 45
    d. 60

    Reference_____

20. Tests requiring a pressure of 10 psig or less shall utilize a testing gauge having increments of _____ psi or less.

    a. 0.05   b. 0.10

    c. 0.50   d. 1.00

Reference_____

21. A gaseous hydrogen system is designed to generate, store and distribute a nontoxic hydrogen gas mixture containing not more than _____ percent oxygen.

    a. 0.5   b. 1.0

    c. 1.5   d. 2.0

Reference_____

22. Tests requiring a pressure greater than 100 psig shall utilize a testing gauge having increments of _____ psi or less.

    a. 0.5   b. 1.0

    c. 2.0   d. 5.0

Reference_____

23. Vent pipe outlets for purging hydrogen piping systems must be located a minimum of _____ feet above the adjacent ground level.

    a. 8   b. 10

    c. 12   d. 15

Reference_____

24. Gases being purged from a hydrogen piping system shall be discharged outdoors and shall be at least _____ feet from building openings and lot lines.

    a. 5   b. 10

    c. 20   d. 30

Reference_____

25. The hydrostatic test pressure on a hydrogen piping system shall be not less than _____ times the maximum working pressure.

    a. 2   b. 3

    c. $1^1/_2$ d. $2^1/_2$

Reference_____

Answer Keys

Study Session 1
2021 *International Fuel Gas Code*

1.	c	Sec. 101.2
2.	a	Sec. 101.2.2
3.	c	Sec. 101.2.4, #4
4.	a	Sec. 101.4
5.	b	Sec. 102.1
6.	d	Sec. 102.2
7.	d	Sec. 102.3
8.	b	Sec. 102.4
9.	c	Sec. 102.5
10.	a	Sec. 102.6
11.	b	Sec. 105.2
12.	b	Sec. 104.3
13.	b	Sec. 104.1
14.	d	Sec. 105.1
15.	c	Sec. 105.2
16.	a	Sec. 105.2.1
17.	b	Sec. 105.3.2
18.	d	Sec. 106.3
19.	b	Sec. 106.2
20.	d	Sec. 106.3.2
21.	c	Sec. 106.5.6
22.	a	Sec. 106.5.8
23.	d	Sec. 110.2
24.	d	Sec. 113.3
25.	a	Sec. 110.3

Study Session 2
2021 *International Fuel Gas Code*

1.	b	Sec. 301.3
2.	c	Sec. 301.3
3.	b	Sec. 301.5
4.	d	Sec. 304.1
5.	c	Sec. 301.7.1
6.	b	Sec. 301.11
7.	d	Sec. 302.3.2
8.	d	Sec. 302.3.1
9.	a	Sec. 302.3.3
10.	d	Sec. 302.6
11.	d	Sec. 303.3, #4
12.	c	Sec. 303.4
13.	d	Sec. 304.3
14.	b	Sec. 304.4
15.	c	Sec. 304.5.1
16.	d	Sec. 304.5.2
17.	a	Sec. 302.3.2
18.	a	Sec. 304.5.3.2
19.	c	Sec. 304.6.1
20.	a	Sec. 304.6
21.	a	Sec. 304.6.2
22.	d	Sec. 304.9
23.	d	Sec. 304.10
24.	c	Sec. 304.11, #1
25.	b	Sec. 304.11, #1, Exc.

Study Session 3
2021 *International Fuel Gas Code*

1.	a	Sec. 305.2
2.	b	Sec. 305.3
3.	c	Sec. 305.4
4.	d	Sec. 305.4
5.	d	Sec. 305.5
6.	c	Sec. 306.4
7.	a	Sec. 306.6, Exc.
8.	b	Sec. 305.7
9.	c	Sec. 306.2
10.	c	Sec. 306.3
11.	a	Sec. 306.3
12.	d	Sec. 306.3.1
13.	b	Sec. 306.5
14.	c	Sec. 306.5.1
15.	a	Sec. 306.6, Exc.
16.	c	Sec. 306.5
17.	d	Sec. 307.3
18.	a	Sec. 307.2
19.	b	Sec. 307.6
20.	a	Sec. 305.7
21.	d	Table 308.2
22.	c	Table 308.2, Note e
23.	c	Table 308.2, Note i
24.	d	Sec. 310.2.2
25.	d	Sec. 310.2.3

Study Session 4
2021 International Fuel Gas Code

1.	a	Sec. 401.5
2.	c	Sec. 401.7
3.	a	Sec. 402.2
4.	b	Sec. 402.3, #2
5.	b	Sec. 402.4.1
6.	a	Sec. 402.7, #5
7.	c	Sec. 403.2
8.	c	Sec. 403.4.3
9.	d	Sec. 403.9.5, #9.2
10.	d	Sec. 403.9.5, #1
11.	b	Sec. 404.3
12.	c	Sec. 403.5
13.	a	Sec. 404.5
14.	a	Sec. 404.6
15.	b	Sec. 404.8.1
16.	c	Sec. 404.8.2
17.	a	Sec. 404.9
18.	a	Sec. 404.12
19.	d	Sec. 404.16
20.	a	Sec. 404.17.1
21.	c	Sec. 404.17.3
22.	c	Sec. 404.5
23.	c	Sec. 406.4.2
24.	d	Sec. 406.4.1
25.	a	Sec. 404.7.1

Study Session 5
2021 *International Fuel Gas Code*

1.	c	Sec. 415.1, Table 415.1
2.	a	Sec. 415.1, Table 415.1
3.	a	Sec. 408.4
4.	a	Sec. 408.4
5.	a	Sec. 409.1.2
6.	b	Sec. 409.3.2
7.	c	Sec. 409.5.1
8.	a	Sec. 409.5.1
9.	d	Sec. 411.1, #8
10.	b	Sec. 409.5.2
11.	d	Sec. 410.3
12.	d	Sec. 409.5.3
13.	a	Sec. 411.1, #3
14.	b	Sec. 409.5.3
15.	b	Sec. 409.6
16.	b	Sec. 410.3, Exc.
17.	b	Sec. 410.2, #7
18.	d	Sec. 408.1
19.	d	Sec. 411.1.6
20.	d	Sec. 412.9, #2
21.	c	Sec. 412.8.2
22.	a	Sec. 413.3.1, #2
23.	b	Sec. 416.1
24.	a	Sec. 413.4.3, #3
25.	c	Sec. 415.1, Table 415.1

Study Session 6
2021 *International Fuel Gas Code*

1. b Sec. 501.1, 501.3
2. c Sec. 501.1
3. a Sec. 501.7.2
4. a Sec. 502.7.1
5. d Sec. 501.9
6. b Sec. 501.10
7. b Sec. 501.15.3
8. a Sec. 501.8
9. c Sec. 502.4
10. b Sec. 502.7
11. a Sec. 502.4
12. a Sec. 501.7.1
13. c Sec. 503.3.3, #5
14. c Sec. 503.6.14
15. b Sec. 503.5.4
16. d Sec. 503.6.5, #1, Fig. 503.6.5
17. c Sec. 503.5.4
18. a Sec. 502.7
19. d Sec. 503.4, Table 503.4
20. c Sec. 503.6.6
21. b Sec. 503.6.5, #1, Fig. 503.6.5
22. b Sec. 503.6.8
23. a Sec. 503.6.5, #2
24. c Sec. 503.6.5.1
25. a Sec. 503.6.11

Study Session 7
2021 *International Fuel Gas Code*

1.	d	Table 503.8
2.	a	Sec. 503.7.3
3.	c	Sec. 503.10.2.2
4.	b	Sec. 503.7.1
5.	b	Sec. 503.7.2
6.	a	Sec. 503.7.3
7.	b	Sec. 503.7.3
8.	d	Sec. 503.7.5
9.	d	Sec. 503.7.6
10.	c	Sec. 503.8
11.	b	Sec. 503.8
12.	d	Sec. 503.8
13.	a	Sec. 503.10.8
14.	c	Sec. 503.10.9
15.	d	Sec. 503.10.9
16.	b	Sec. 503.10.2.5, Table 503.10.2.5
17.	b	Sec. 503.12.5
18.	a	Sec. 503.10.5, Table 502.10.5
19.	d	Sec. 503.12.7
20.	a	Sec. 504.2.11, 504.3.21
21.	c	Sec. 504.3.7
22.	b	Sec. 505.1.1
23.	d	Sec. 503.8
24.	a	Sec. 504.3.2, Table 504.3.2
25.	b	Sec. 503.10.5, Table 503.10.5

Study Session 8
2021 *International Fuel Gas Code*

1. c Sec. 608.4
2. b Sec. 608.5
3. d Sec. 609.2, #3
4. b Sec. 609.2, #2
5. b Sec. 609.2, #2
6. a Sec. 609.2, #4
7. a Sec. 609.4
8. a Sec. 609.4
9. b Sec. 612.5
10. d Sec. 614.4
11. d Sec. 614.8
12. c Sec. 614.9.2
13. c Sec. 614.4
14. a Sec. 614.7
15. d Sec. 614.7.1
16. c Sec. 614.9.1
17. b Sec. 614.9.2
18. c Sec. 614.8
19. a Sec. 614.8
20. c Sec. 614.9.5
21. c Sec. 614.9.4.3
22. a Sec. 614.9.4.1, Table 614.9.4.1
23. c Sec. 614.10
24. d Sec. 614.11, #10
25. c Sec. 614.11, #7

Study Session 9
2021 *International Fuel Gas Code*

1.	b	Sec. 615.6
2.	a	Sec. 615.7
3.	b	Sec. 618.3, #7
4.	d	Sec. 618.2
5.	c	Sec. 618.2
6.	d	Sec. 618.3, #1
7.	d	Sec. 618.5
8.	c	Sec. 618.3, #6
9.	d	Sec. 620.2
10.	c	Sec. 620.4
11.	c	Sec. 621.3
12.	a	Sec. 621.4
13.	a	Sec. 621.6
14.	c	Sec. 623.3
15.	d	Sec. 623.5.1
16.	c	Sec. 623.7
17.	b	Sec. 623.7, #1
18.	b	Sec. 624.2
19.	a	Sec. 615.7.1
20.	d	Sec. 615.6
21.	b	Sec. 627.10
22.	c	Sec. 620.4
23.	c	Sec. 628.3
24.	a	Sec. 630.3
25.	b	Sec. 615.6.1

Study Session 10
2021 *International Fuel Gas Code*

1. c Sec. 703.3.7
2. b Sec. 703.1
3. b Sec. 702.1
4. c Sec. 703.2.1
5. b Sec. 705.3.2
6. c Sec. 704.1.2.3.4
7. b Sec. 704.2
8. a Sec. 704.1.2.2, #4
9. d Sec. 703.3.1
10. d Sec. 704.1.2
11. d Sec. 704.1.2.2, #2
12. c Sec. 704.1.2.3
13. a Sec. 705.3.2
14. c Sec. 704.1.2.4.1
15. d Sec. 704.1.2.4.2
16. c Sec. 705.2
17. b Sec. 705.3.1
18. a Sec. 704.1.2.4
19. b Sec. 705.3.5
20. b Sec. 705.3.6, #1
21. b Sec. 702.1
22. c Sec. 705.3.6, #3
23. a Sec. 705.5.3.1
24. a Sec. 705.5.3.1
25. c Sec. 705.3.1

ASSESSMENT center

The ICC Assessment Center (formerly known as ICC Certification & Testing) provides nationally recognized credentials that demonstrate a confirmed commitment to protect public health, safety, and welfare. Raise the professionalism of your department and further your career by pursuing an ICC Certification.

ICC Certifications offer:

- Nationwide recognition
- Increased earning potential
- Career advancement
- Superior knowledge
- Validation of your expertise
- Personal and professional satisfaction

Exams are developed and maintained to the highest standards, which includes continuous peer review by national committees of experienced, practicing professionals. ICC is continually evolving exam offerings, testing options, and technology to ensure that all building and fire safety officials have access to the tools and resources needed to advance in today's fast-paced and rapidly-changing world.

Enhancing Exam Options

Effective July 2018, the Assessment Center enhanced and streamlined exam options and now offers only computer based testing (CBT) at a test site and PRONTO. We no longer offer paper/pencil exams.

Proctored Remote Online Testing Option (PRONTO)

Taking your next ICC certification exam is more convenient, more comfortable and more efficient than ever before with PRONTO.

PRONTO provides a convenient testing experience that is accessible 24 hours a day, 7 days a week, 365 days a year. Required hardware/software is minimal – you will need a webcam and microphone, as well as a reasonably recent operating system.

Whether testing in your office or in the comfort of your home, your ICC exam will continue to maintain its credibility while offering more convenience, allowing you to focus on achieving your professional goals. The Assessment Center continues to add exams to the PRONTO exam catalog regularly.

18-15617

Checkout all the ICC Assessment Center has to offer at iccsafe.org/certification

Training and Education

The Learning Center at ICC has the training opportunities you need to advance your career and earn valuable CEUs!

 CLASSROOM Attend a live training event in person or virtually.
- Residential Building Inspector – B1 Certification Test Academy
- Residential Mechanical Inspector – M1 Certification Test Academy
- Residential Plumbing Inspector – P1 Certification Test Academy
- Getting the Most of the IPMC®
- IMC® Design, Installation and Inspection Principles
- IPC® Backflow Prevention and Cross Connection Control Requirements
- IPC Design, Installation and Inspection Principles
- IPC Essentials
- IPC/IMC®/IFGC® Significant Changes
- IRC® Performing Residential Plumbing Inspections

LIVE WEB SESSION
- IPC Webinar Series
- IMC Webinar Series
- IPMC Webinar Series
- IFGC Webinar Series

 ONLINE Online learning is available 24/7 and features topics such as exam study, code training, management, and leadership.

 HIRE ICC TO TEACH ICC will bring the training to you. We can customize the training to meet the needs of your organization.
Subject matter examples include:
- IPC® Design, Installation and Inspection Principles
- IMC® Design, Installation and Inspection Principles
- IFGC® Design Installation and Inspection Principles

Check out our Class Schedule at **learn.iccsafe.org** today or call **888-422-7233, x33821** for more information!

ICC EVALUATION SERVICE

ICC-ES PMG is the leading provider of product evaluations in plumbing, mechanical and fuel gas - with excellent customer service and the highest acceptability by code officials, at the price you're looking for.

We certify:
- Faucets
- Showerheads
- Bathtubs
- Sink products
- Toilets & Urinals
- Ceramic Fixtures
- Resins and Linear Drain products

and many more!

Benefits of having an ICC-ES PMG Listing:

- ICC-ES PMG offers a **lower cost** for certification than competitors
- Expedited certification for all client listings
- ICC-ES PMG **does not conduct warehouse inspections**
- ICC-ES PMG **does not charge for additional company listings**

- ICC-ES will accept test reports from other entities
- **No fee for EPA WaterSense listings and lead law listings**
- **No separate file for NSF 61 listings**
- A2LA, ANSI, SCC and EMA accreditation

www.icc-es.org/pmg
800-423-6587 x7643

Valuable Guides to Changes in the 2021 I-Codes®

SIGNIFICANT CHANGES TO THE 2021 INTERNATIONAL CODES®

Practical resources that offer a comprehensive analysis of the critical changes made between the 2018 and 2021 editions of the codes. Authored by ICC code experts, these useful tools are "must-have" guides to the many important changes in the 2021 International Codes.

Key changes are identified then followed by in-depth, expert discussion of how the change affects real world application. A full-color photo, table or illustration is included for each change to further clarify application.

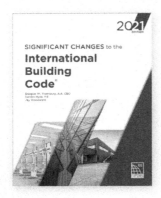

SIGNIFICANT CHANGES TO THE IBC®, 2021 EDITION
#7024S21

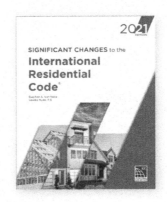

SIGNIFICANT CHANGES TO THE IRC®, 2021 EDITION
#7101S21

SIGNIFICANT CHANGES TO THE IFC®, 2021 EDITION
#7404S21

SIGNIFICANT CHANGES TO THE IPC®/IMC®/IFGC®, 2021 EDITION
#7202S21

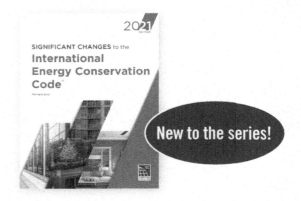

SIGNIFICANT CHANGES TO THE IECC®, 2021 EDITION
#7808S21

New to the series!

Order Your Helpful Guides Today! 1-800-786-4452 | www.iccsafe.org/books